Growing Up into the Children of God

Exploring the Paradoxes of Christian Maturity

— DAVID NEWMAN —

Sacristy
Press

Sacristy Press
PO Box 612, Durham, DH1 9HT

www.sacristy.co.uk

First published in 2019 by Sacristy Press, Durham

Sacristy Limited, registered in England & Wales, number 7565667

British Library Cataloguing-in-Publication Data
A catalogue record for the book is available from the British Library

ISBN 978-1-78959-020-3

My heart is not proud, Lord,
my eyes are not haughty;
I do not concern myself with great matters
or things too wonderful for me.
But I have calmed and quieted myself.
I am like a weaned child with its mother;
like a weaned child I am content.

Psalm 131:1–2

Lay aside immaturity and live, and walk in the way of insight.

Proverbs 9:6 (NRSV)

Contents

Acknowledgements

If it takes a village to bring up a child it has certainly taken a community of family, friends, colleagues and mentors to experience, reflect on and write about growing up. I am grateful to so many people. Thanks to my good friend David Runcorn for asking the question that helped conceive the idea. Thanks to Simon Kingston for encouragement and advice when the project was going wobbly. Thanks to Rosemary Langford-Bellaby for support and insight over many years. But most of all thank-you to my family—to Hannah, Becky and Tim for enduring my parenting and for being such a source of delight, learning and inspiration. Thanks Tim too for your patient proof-reading and for being so much more grammatically correct than your father; to Andrew for designing the lovely cover; and finally to Helen—whose love and faithful partnership has been the gift that has made my own journey possible and ultimately so happy and creative.

Introduction

My parents never moved from the house where we all grew up, so when my father died at the age of 96, clearing the house became quite an adventure of discovery. He was a bit of a hoarder and the house had several spare rooms and a large loft, so cases and files of paper kept emerging—letters, bills, receipts, business documents, all sorts of paraphernalia from sixty years of living there—and then, rather scarily, most of our school reports. They confirmed the memory for me of when I was sixteen and a report had arrived home at the end of term, with a rather unsettling comment from the headmaster. Usually he wrote a few bland generalizations at the end of the other teachers' more detailed comments. But this time the words were much more direct and disturbing: "He's not going to like this, but I think it's about time that David grew up . . . "

He was right, I didn't like it, and I remember feeling that adolescent mixture of anger and anxiety. I had clearly messed up but there didn't seem to be much guidance as to what I could do about it. I couldn't just say I was sorry that I'd forgotten to grow up, in the same way I might have failed to hand in an essay or revise for an exam. In fact, it didn't feel like something that was completely in my hands. Growing up was very dependent on significant others, on affirmation, respect, and constructive criticism. Moreover, although they were not consciously articulated at the time, I was left with many questions. "What did 'growing up' actually mean?" "Was it just being like 'grown-ups', and if so was that actually a good thing?" "Was it something that you had some control over, or did it just happen in response to life's circumstances?" "Is growing up something you arrive at, or is it a never-ending process?"

I tell that story, not just to introduce myself through a snatch of my own experience, but because it points up the central questions of this book. What is human maturity, and in particular, in what ways does that relate to God? Of course, there are those who would answer the second part of the question with, "Not at all". Faith in God is seen as immaturity, a failure to grow up and take proper responsibility. The so-called "new atheists" trumpet the immaturity of faith in the face of the grown-up rationality of science. So Richard Dawkins asserts:

> There is something infantile in the presumption that somebody else (parents in the case of children, God in the case of adults) has a responsibility to give your life meaning and point. It is all of a piece with the infantilism of those who, the moment they twist their ankle, look around for someone to sue. Somebody else must be responsible for my well-being, and somebody else must be to blame if I am hurt. Is it a similar infantilism that really lies behind the "need" for a God? . . . The truly adult view, by contrast, is that our life is as meaningful, as full and as wonderful as we choose to make it.[1]

I want to contest their essential premise on the grounds that I do not see it as infantile to own that we will always have needs, and maturity is not to be invulnerable or completely self-sufficient. A stage of growing up may include an assertion of independence from the innocent or naive dependencies of the early years, but that can never be the finished article. If we are made for relationship, then maturity will be a capacity for interdependence, to be able to give and receive according to our gifts and needs. Our Western culture has encouraged a more detached individualism, but there are different perspectives in other cultures. For instance, the South African philosophy of "Ubuntu" emphasizes interconnectedness—"I am because you are." Within that there is every space for God—"We are because He is."

However, I do concede that the new atheists pose a challenge to faith and organized religion. They pose the question, "Are they real and responsible, particularly in the face of the hard questions and issues of life?" Where faith in God is maintained by avoiding pain and darkness, by peddling certainties rather than owning complexity, or by a lack of responsible engagement with the world, then that faith remains immature and essentially precarious. These are issues for many I encounter in the church—especially for those "expectant" disciples for whom God has not quite "turned up" as much as they once hoped for, and who find themselves feeling easily disillusioned by the worship and the beliefs that shape those expectations. It is also an important question for those very responsible churchgoers who have just got a bit weary in their Christian service. The first of these can appear not "grown-up" enough, wanting God to do everything for them when a bit more adult responsibility would seem healthy. The second can appear too "grown-up" in their faith, with a spirituality that is often very centred on duty—captured in a memorable line from a Cat Stevens song, " . . . doing the work of God trying to make things better for Him".[2] I long for them to know more of the freedom and joy of being children of God.

The first of these groups seem a particular issue within evangelical/ Pentecostal/charismatic (EPC) churches, the tradition which has most shaped my own spiritual journey and which has been the growing part of the church (numerically) in the last half-century. As Alan Jamieson notes, "while EPC churches are growing rapidly, it appears, at least in the West, that these same churches also have a wide-open back door through which the disgruntled, disillusioned and disaffected leave."[3] Some hang on within the church but know a growing dissonance between the bold and excited expressions of their worship and life as it really is. Some join the growing number of those who describe themselves as "spiritual but not religious" and continue on a meaningful faith journey, alone or with others but separated from the mainstream church. Some end up leaving church altogether and joining the ranks of the "de-churched".[4] There will no doubt be those who describe such a journey as simple backsliding and a loss of faith. However, my sense is that people are left spiritually vulnerable because their understanding of God has not kept in step with their experience of life, and they end up leaving the church when the gulf becomes too wide. My conviction is that such disillusionment and the consequent exodus from church is not inevitable.

Growing Up into the Children of God is written with such people in mind, through exploring ways of articulating and understanding the paradoxes of believing, and incorporating them into a growing faith. My aim is to enable a child-like faith while rejecting childish patterns of thought. In some respects, this is a dialogue between the generations at a time when churches are increasingly demarcated by age. As an archdeacon in the Church of England, it was not uncommon for me to visit churches where I was the youngest present; but if on a spare Sunday I slipped into a nearby "new church", I was certainly among the oldest. The traditional denominations are increasingly populated by the older generation—the average age of an Anglican worshipper is 62—while the under forties are more likely to be found in one of the new churches rather than the historic denominations. If a grown-up faith involves a journey of different stages, are these inevitably contained either in different congregations or beyond any formal church at all? How does a church attract the beginner but retain the mature? Does the generation gap in the church simply mirror that in the world?

This book is also a dialogue between the evangelical/charismatic and liberal wings of the church, which seeks to explore the interface between the divine and human components of faith, between revelation and reason, God and the world. This dialogue has had a particular intensity since Dietrich Bonhoeffer articulated phrases like "man come of age" and "religionless Christianity" in his writing from prison, in the final months of the Second World War. Bonhoeffer was pointing out that in a world of increasing scientific and technological sophistication (and this was seventy-five years ago!), creating a narrow understanding of God was inadequate, and the arena of biblical faith had to be the whole of life and not some religious sub-section. However, he could be heard as suggesting that humankind had grown up beyond its need of God and the church. Since then a succession of liberal/evangelical or radical/traditional controversies have erupted—the *Honest to God* debate in the sixties, the *Myth of God Incarnate* in the seventies, the Bishop of Durham and the resurrection in the eighties, and the "Sea of Faith" (inspired by Don Cupitt). These tensions surface today in the debates on gender and sexuality.

Such polarities were all too real in my experience when in 1997 I moved to Loughborough as a church leader, and found two very distinct groups of churches, split along these theological fault-lines. A "Sea of Faith" group of clergy from the town had received prominence through a BBC *Heart of the Matter* programme in which they had purportedly denied the resurrection of Jesus. (There was a time when every Easter, it seemed, some church leader was given publicity on such lines.) It was, of course, more subtle than that, but nonetheless, the thrust of the

"Sea of Faith" position was a "non-realist" view of God, whereby God is essentially a human creation giving expression to our transcendent values and meanings. In shocked reaction, evangelical leaders and their churches had withdrawn from any association with such leaders. Furthermore, they distanced themselves from those not necessarily holding such views but who associated with those who did, within the Churches Together forum. Clear and certain orthodoxy for them had become the prerequisite of fellowship. The unfortunate consequence was a divided mission in the town that would have been much stronger with at least some reconciled diversity. However, the space to explore that mix of the divine and human that constitutes a mature faith was lost.

In Loughborough we did manage to move on from those divides, and a new and exciting Churches Partnership was formed, incorporating most of the churches in the town. That may have been the result of the arrival of new people, but I think it also reflected how times were changing. Up to then, the debate had been around the possibility of the supernatural and an intervening God. However, often the ground of the debate was still what was rational or reasonable. So there would be a marshalling of facts by both sides—scientific facts that would challenge the claims of faith, or religious or historical facts that would support them. So when evangelicals wanted to affirm the physical resurrection of Jesus, they would seek rational proofs in a forensic way, presenting the evidence as in a court of law. At the same time, liberals would point up the difficulties of a God who intervened in the world and did "knock-down physical miracles" in some situations while remaining seemingly passive in others.

However, culture was changing. In the so-called "postmodern era" personal experience was becoming much more important, with the understanding that not everything could be reduced simply to rational explanation. Truth could not be reduced merely to facts. Spirituality of many kinds was coming onto the agenda and people talked of the "re-enchantment of life". In many respects it is a more hospitable climate for faith. The danger now is less that people will not believe anything, but that they will believe everything. God is one option on a whole menu of personal beliefs and experiences. Perhaps that particular pendulum will start to swing back again as the implications of a "post-truth" culture become evident, and "alternative facts" or "fake news" reveal a new irrationality.

These are interesting times, and it is not clear what vision of maturity will emerge from this ferment or what place God will have within it. Certainly the controversies in the church are as fierce as ever. While the Church of England (and the Anglican Communion) has just about negotiated the issue of women in leadership, it faces the real possibility of schism over human sexuality. Alternative bishops are being consecrated, alternative synods arranged, and lines in the sand are being drawn. Angela Tilby touched a raw nerve when she described her response to the prayer initiative "Thy Kingdom Come" as, "I shall be praying for an escape from the Evangelical takeover of the Church", going on to complain that, "Too often in church, people in distress are patronised by the saved and the certain, infantilised by a faux inclusivity."[5] A curt response came the following week from reader and churchwarden Dennis Croome: "How sad! She clearly has not realised that, if Evangelicals left the Church of England, there would be very little left."[6] The question remains. Are conservatives and radicals, evangelicals and liberals bound to divide, or is there a model for a believing and responsible faith that can respect the diversity?

It has been the Pentecostal/charismatic churches that have witnessed growth in recent years, with their openness to a lively and experiential spirituality. I certainly value the experience of God found in many EPC churches, which has renewed both faith and vocation in the church at this time when there is suspicion of institutions and a diminishing commitment to organized religion. It is the setting that has initiated and nurtured my own faith.

However, if such a faith is going to sustain people and transform communities, it has to connect with the real world—with its amazing potential and frightening darkness, with joy and depression, generosity and cruelty. Contemporary knowledge and experience have to be integrated with the way we understand God. I am seeking to do that through the extended metaphor of "grown-up children", which for me has been a helpful model for exploring a mature faith. That faith needs to find the path between certainty and unbelief, between turning God into a magician or just attaching religious language to an essentially human enterprise. I believe that it is possible to retain a belief in a real God who acts in the world, and also to be true to the reality of human experience, especially the reality of suffering and death. However, it may mean jettisoning some unhelpful understandings of God on the way.

I will define what I mean by "grown-up children" more fully in the coming pages, and explain how I am using the metaphor. For me it expresses the paradoxical nature of growing. In the natural world, growth just happens automatically, as Jesus points out in parables:

> A man scatters seed on the ground. Night and day, whether he
> sleeps or gets up, the seed sprouts and grows, though he does not
> know how. *All by itself* the soil produces corn . . .
> > *Mark 4:26–28 (my italics)*

Yet even here there is a human part—sowing, tending, reaping—so that although human action cannot produce growth, it can certainly encourage or prevent it, and it is necessary to understand what is the natural (or divine) part and what the human.

Paradoxes abound in the New Testament: "losing your life in order to find it" (Matthew 16:25), "when I am weak then I am strong" (2 Corinthians 12:10), "I worked harder than all of them—yet not I, but the grace of God that was with me" (1 Corinthians 15:10). They seek to express the mystery of life and growth coming from beyond us, and yet also involving our actions. The metaphor of grown-up children also contains something of that mystery, of how maturity is an increasing acceptance of a reality that is given from beyond us, but which is also shaped by us. Understanding the nature of that human responsibility is key to growing up. We have been given the capacity to think things through, to make choices, to take action. A naive idealism, laziness, or projecting the blame on to another can all be signs of an unwillingness to grow up. Yet paradoxically, maturity is also realizing the limits of responsibility. It acknowledges our dependencies and need of others.

When my son was very small, we were reflecting at bedtime one night on the events of the day, which for him had involved time at playgroup. He suddenly looked at me and said, "Daddy, you're not little enough to go on the big slide." I think it was his revenge for all the occasions we had said to him when he wanted to do something, "Well, you're not big enough to do that yet." So he had worked out something that you had to be little to do. Maturity involves being little enough and big enough in appropriate ways. One of the paradoxes Jesus articulates in the Gospels is how we need to be little enough to understand spiritual reality, how things are hidden from the wise and learned and revealed to little children.[7] Yet we also need to be big enough to think robustly and act responsibly.

I don't know precisely what my headmaster envisaged when he challenged me to grow up. I am sure he wouldn't have wanted to suppress completely the searching, sometimes anxious, sometimes flippant, sometimes rebellious adolescent that I was. I'm sure I must have been annoying and frustrating at times. Maybe he wanted to scare me into reaching my potential in a more disciplined and tolerant way. However, I wish he had been able to express a bit more sense of support for one who was clearly struggling with some of the more scary steps of growing responsibility.

The point is that we all come to the business of growing up with a mixture of needs and gifts, strength and weakness. Self-help can only get us so far—as will a passive dependence on others. I believe that a right relationship with God creates the space for human flourishing, but that too is about the right interdependence. I passionately long for a grown-up church with grown-up Christians having an impact on the world. I have come to understand this maturity as the outworking of an interdependent divine-human partnership, which might be described from a human point of view as being grown-up children. This book seeks to portray what that might mean, so that we may enter more fully into the paradox of growing up into the children of God.

For further thought and discussion

- Is growing up a good thing?
- As you read the introduction, note anything that excites you, puzzles you, or challenges you. You might want to mark these with a "☺" or a "?" or a "!". Talk about your responses.
- "I have come to understand this maturity as the outworking of an interdependent divine-human partnership." How, in your experience, would you describe that partnership?
- Read 1 Corinthians 15:9–11. How does Paul describe the divine and human elements in his own ministry?

CHAPTER 1

On growing up . . .

Growing up is an expression full of different meanings and emotions for different people. Sometimes it means no more than growing older, although most realize that the two are not the same. Being told to "grow up" is usually an insult or rebuke for infantile behaviour, and yet being grown-up can sound rather dull and boring in some contexts. Sometimes we expect it to happen intensely at particular moments—as in our use of "adolescence", a general word based on the Latin for growing up but having the connotation of a particular stage of childhood in our usage. Society will denote particular ages for "coming of age"—twenty-one, eighteen, sixteen—and generally we look ahead at older people imagining great maturity, and cannot believe, when we get there, how young we still feel.

Most of the associations with adolescence suggest a time of turbulence and conflict. Someone has described the "terrible twos" as the first adolescence, when a toddler can express the fears and frustrations of their initial steps of independence in tantrums of real rage. It is a rehearsal for the real thing a few years later as young people cross the narrow bridge between childhood and adulthood, one moment terrified by its freedom and responsibilities, the next frustrated by continuing restrictions either from without or within. It is also difficult for parents, who can feel completely deskilled and humiliated by these emerging superstars who can do anything and everything better than they can, a process which modern technology has made especially sharp and cruel. Mark Twain is reputed to have said, "When I was a boy of fourteen, my father was so ignorant I could hardly stand to have the old man around. But when I got to be twenty-one, I was astonished at how much he had learned in seven years." Maybe it's always been like that, but parents will have some sympathy for the person who said that adolescence is nature's way of preparing for the empty nest.

If growing up is more than just ageing, then we need some vision of maturity, some awareness of the goal of the process. In the musical *Matilda* there is a wonderful song in which the children imagine what life will be like "When I grow up". Some of it is throwing off the perceived restrictions to the enjoyment of life, like eating sweets every day. However, there is also the circular vision of growing up in order to enable you to be a grown-up—being tall enough to reach the branches of the trees that grown-ups need to climb, being strong enough to carry the heavy things that grown-ups need to carry. They are reassuring themselves that they will have new powers to meet adult responsibilities. However, there is also the sense of these children longing just to have power itself, to be in control of their lives. It is entirely understandable, given their oppressive circumstances. Yet it begs the question, "Power for what?" In the musical we enjoy their spirited rebellion. In real life, we know that today's victims can become tomorrow's persecutors if that question is not answered.

Psychological and spiritual maturity

Psychologists have their different prescriptions for the mature, grown-up life, but typical concepts are self-awareness and acceptance, warm and non-competitive relationships with others, a capacity to cope with life, correct perceptions of reality, creativity and humour, spontaneity and gratitude, integrity, and some sort of philosophy of life. It is an interesting question as to whether spiritual and psychological maturity are the same thing. Certainly some of the great saints have not always been the most balanced people, and prophetic types can be found on the margins of life, socially and psychologically. It seems that great insights, passions, and deeds can emerge from our wounds and deprivations. The same could be said about creative people—and even about some who have been outstanding leaders. When it comes to genius, living on the edge of sanity, or at least psychological maturity, has sometimes been the reality. The insights of the madman and the fool are a common theme in literature. When the prevailing behaviours of a culture have become evil and oppressive, then it may be the dissidents and deviants that offer the truly mature voice. Faith can sometimes challenge our perceptions of normality.

However, the fact that God can use everything, even our lack of wholeness, does not mean we should drive a wedge between spiritual and more general human maturity. Peter Scazzero wrote a helpful book called *Emotionally Healthy Spirituality*, with the subtitle, "It's impossible to be spiritually mature while remaining emotionally immature."[8] Our relationship with God does not bypass our humanity, and our growth towards maturity will often mean revisiting the patterns and norms of behaviour we have inherited in our upbringing, along with the wounds we have received on the way. A faith centred on the incarnation, on the truth that God became human, should alert us to this reality, and many Christians will want to start with Jesus Christ as a model of true personhood. "Here is the man," said Pontius Pilate as Jesus was brought out in the regal attire of purple robe and crown of thorns, and believers have been happy to hear a truth that transcended Pilate's wearily ironical tone: "Here is the real man, here is a sight of true humanity."

Jesus growing up

The problem is that the New Testament gives us only a limited sight of that humanity, certainly in terms of growing up, which can make maturity appear a rather narrowly religious or moral idea rather than more generally human. The epistles concentrate mainly on the significance of Jesus' life, death, and resurrection for the life of faith, and even the more narrative Gospels contain virtually nothing about Jesus' childhood or young adulthood, leaping almost straight from the infancy narratives to the beginning of his ministry. Certainly we can infer much about maturity from his adult life, but less about growing up—at least not through narrative example. As a result, the moralistic, behaviour-orientated type of sentiment, "Christian children all must be / mild, obedient, good as he", has tended to dominate the field.[9]

However, there is *one* chapter in the Gospels which refers to some of Jesus' life between birth and adult ministry, and that is Luke 2. True, it contains only two stories after the birth itself: one just a month or so later, and the other when Jesus was twelve. However, each is specifically linked with the maturing process, as at the end of both stories Luke writes a summarizing conclusion: "And the child grew and became strong; he was filled with wisdom, and the grace of God was on him." (v.40); "And Jesus increased in wisdom and in years, and in divine and human favour." (v.52, NRSV). Here was a boy maturing in a holistic way, physically and mentally, spiritually and socially, and the implication is that what happens in these stories is connected to that maturity.

The importance of intergenerational relationships

The first is the moving story of when Jesus, as a baby, was presented in the temple by his parents. There's a lot of joy in this story. The older ones— Simeon and Anna, one at least in her eighties—are joyfully at peace. Seeing this young family, they are ready to die feeling fulfilled, thankful, and full of hope. The young couple are filled with expectation and wonder, marvelling at what they are told about their baby. Across the generations, each is the source of the other's joy. The older generation are thrilled with the promise of the young family before them. They have been utterly committed to pray and prepare for God's purposes to be worked out through those coming after them, and now they believe they are seeing it. The young family have begun to sense not just the responsibility of being parents for the first time, but of nurturing a child with a special destiny and purpose. A daunting and demanding role lies ahead of them, but this older couple have encouraged them to believe that it would be possible and that, no matter what the cost, they will be used by God for something very special. Old and young are crucial to each other's joy. From this mature partnership of young and old comes a maturing child—growing physically, growing in wisdom, growing in the grace of God.

As we have said, churches today are increasingly demarcated by age or by attitude. Often the older people are saying, "We just want it how it used to be," "We want what we're used to," while the younger people are saying, "Traditional church is so last century . . . so boring." Sadly, the church often reflects the manufactured discontent of a consumer society that increasingly drives a wedge between the generations with the speed of change and fashion. We struggle to offer something prophetic and countercultural, and get caught up in a classic adolescent battle where "Nothing's right," "They're impossible," "We need more respect," "If only they did this," and so on. The characters in this story offer a challenge to both generations, young and old.

First of all, Simeon and Anna are so faithfully forward-looking. As we get older it's much easier to be backward-looking, to hark back to perceived golden times when churches were well attended and music was familiarly traditional, and families came to church and sat quietly through the services, or whatever (although they do say that nostalgia is not what it used to be . . .)! These two are quite the opposite. They are looking forward—Simeon, it says, was "waiting for the consolation of Israel", and Anna "gave thanks to God and spoke about the child to all who were looking forward to the redemption of Jerusalem". You sense that their attitude had infected a whole group, enabling them to be expectant and forward-looking. There would have been plenty to grumble about, much cause for discouragement, years of waiting for the prophetic hopes of long ago to be realized while languishing under Roman occupation. Those hopes could have seemed as far off as ever, and it would have been easy to lose faith. But they hadn't, and their faith was infectious.

They are rewarded as Mary and Joseph arrive in the temple with their young baby. They would have come simply out of obedience to the law of Moses, fulfilling the customs of redeeming the firstborn son who was holy to the Lord, and of completing the mother's rites of purification. Today they might have come for a christening or thanksgiving. They offered a pair of doves (or two young pigeons), which was the poor person's sacrifice, the second dove or pigeon taking the place of the more expensive lamb. So they were pretty ordinary, vulnerable, no doubt full of that combination of excitement and anxiety that young parents easily feel. They might have wondered what these old rituals added to their lives, demanding such interruption to their routines, and no doubt some expense. Yet they commit to this act of consecrating the firstborn male, which was the law's way of pointing out priorities: first things were given to the Lord, whether offspring or fruits of the harvest, as a demonstration of gratitude and obedient acknowledgement of grace.

They are rewarded too. When they arrive at the temple, they encounter welcome and encouragement and the discernment of vocation—for in this ordinary, poor family, Anna and Simeon discern the mighty work of God about to be revealed to all people, Gentile and Jew alike, thereby going beyond the scope of anything that the people of God had yet seen or experienced. Two dedicated and obedient young people are met by two faithful and forward-looking old people, and great things are set in train. How encouraging for the young couple to be assured of the prayers of these older ones, and to be given the vision that they had. How encouraging for Simeon and Anna to see the fulfilment of their life's longing and prayer. How much it seems they had to give each other. It is very significant that a chapter about Jesus growing up begins with this very clear meeting of old and young. Contrary to our increasing tendency to segregate young and old, this story points to the importance of that partnership in the road to maturity.

In his wonderfully insightful book *Contemplative Youth Ministry*, Mark Yaconelli tells the story of visiting a church where such a partnership was being lived out in a powerfully creative way. He notices how moved one elderly woman was as she gave out communion to a group of teenagers, to the extent of struggling to keep her composure. After the service he comments to her about how well she must know them, and to his surprise finds out that she has hardly met any of them before. However, she had been part of a scheme whereby older people had served the youth ministry by committing to pray for the young people through exchanging cards with their photos on. She had done this daily for three years, and then on that particular morning, the first time she had assisted at communion, there they all were in front of her, and she was just overwhelmed at handing them the bread of Christ.

Not surprisingly with such prayerful, welcoming adults, young people were attracted to that church. One fifteen-year-old described his experience like this:

> When I leave my house to go to church I usually begin walking like I walk to school. But then as I come around my block and see the church building I start smiling. And by the time I reach the kerb in front of the church, I'm giggling. And then when I reach

the front door of the church, I'm just about ready to fall down laughing because I know as soon as I open that door all of these older folks are going to look over and see me and start smiling. Then they're going to come over and hug me and they're going to ask me all kinds of questions and they're going to want me to sit by them in the service. And that just cracks me up.[10]

Clearly the spirit of what happened in the temple to the holy family lived on in that church. I wonder in how many churches that is true.

It is a huge challenge today to be an intergenerational church. Postmodern consumer culture has bred an "It must fit me" expectation that is impatient with different lifestyles and attitudes and experiences. Mobility and social media encourage a network society where relationships cohere around the like-minded rather than the diverse. The gap between the generations in terms of styles of worship, music, forms of communication, and modes of relating has become ever wider. There is a "crisis in mutual society".[11] As a result, it is argued that we have to accept monocultural expressions of church if we are going to reach different groups of people. It is said that churches will only grow when the "homogeneous unit principle" is accepted—that crossing the threshold of faith is a big enough challenge without having to cross big cultural divides as well. This particularly applies generationally, so that younger and older generations are best catered for in separate units.

There is certainly a force to this argument, and yet it seems to fly in the face of a biblical vision for a multicultural, intergenerational church. Some churches have tried, therefore, to blend two models—by having services (or even parts of services) that cater for different groups, but joining in other ways—or by having mission communities that are more monocultural within a larger church. Certainly, where there is a genuine missional motivation to such demarcation (rather than a prevailing culture wanting to preserve its identity), it can be a creative and necessary force for growth. Yet even within the school that promoted the homogeneous principle there is an admission that this can only be a "penultimate spiritual dynamic" as against the ultimate principle that all are one in the church, and "the more this is manifested in a tangible way, the better."[12]

In an increasingly fragmented world, it is moving to hear of examples of intergenerational relationships that have been mutually enriching. A Dutch nursing home offers university students free accommodation in return for a variety of activities with the older residents, including watching sports, celebrating birthdays, and—perhaps most importantly— offering company when residents fall ill, which helps stave off feelings of disconnectedness both ways. School classes are taken on visits to care homes. So maybe the church needs to be bolder in working out the possibilities and parameters of an intergenerational fellowship. A Channel 5 programme—*Bad Habits, Holy Orders*—boldly followed five young women, variously addicted to alcohol, partying, sex, and social media, to a convent where they stayed for a month. The social, cultural, and generational divides could not have been starker. Yet it was profoundly moving to see the interactions and changes that emerged as the girls and the nuns were able to go beyond the surface and relate in their common humanity. There is certainly a biblical case for saying that if we want mature Christians we must not be content with a monogenerational church.

The rocky bridge of adolescence

The second story in Luke 2 is a real story of adolescence. At the age of 12, Jesus decides to extend the family Passover holiday in Jerusalem without telling his parents, and it's only at the end of a day's travelling that they discover he's not in the party. It takes another day to make tracks back to the city, and so it's not until the third day that they eventually find him engrossed in conversation with the teachers in the temple. His mother's comments have an edge born of anxiety—"Son, why have you treated us like this?"—while Jesus has the casual nonchalance of the unbothered adolescent: "Why were you searching for me? Didn't you know I had to be in my Father's house?" (v.49). We would love to know more. Where did he sleep and eat those two nights? When would he have gone home? Was he really so chilled and matter-of-fact about the whole thing, or was it a more conscious rebellion—or at least a bid for freedom? We are not told. What is clear is that in Jesus' eyes, growing up may have involved asserting some sort of independence from his parents, but it did not stop him continuing to use the language of being a child. He was in *"my Father's* house" (my italics). Something of the experience of childhood was being maintained, but in a new dimension which was adult and spiritual. Indeed, later in his teaching Jesus would turn "growing up" on its head when he said to adults, " . . . unless you change and become like little children, you will never enter the kingdom of heaven." (Matthew 18:3). Some aspects of being a child were to be left behind, but not everything; childlikeness was to be a prerequisite of spiritual maturity.

These stories also suggest that growing up is not pain-free. While it may be possible to negotiate life's maturing transitions in a calm, unruffled manner, or even with joy and excitement, it seems far more common for them to be—to some extent—turbulent or even traumatic. In adolescence young people hover in that uncertain in-between world spanning childhood and adulthood. They still have childhood needs to be met (as indeed do adults) but it is harder to admit that, as it seems a betrayal of the strengthening need for independence and the assertion of a distinct identity. Then there's the question of *which* identity. There will be the conformist identity that has served well enough to maintain the parental relationships the child has needed. Now, though, other models will be competing through peers, teachers, and youth leaders, and new expressions of identity will need testing. That testing can provoke a reaction which is painful, as Jesus found in the temple, and some may opt for the quiet life or assume some sort of "false self" to make life easier.

For adolescent young people do make adults anxious. If even Jesus had that effect on his parents, then we can hardly expect otherwise. Parents have had to settle for an identity to get on with the business of life, and it can be hard to have that questioned. They know some of the dangers that lie in wait for experience-seeking teenagers, and they are protective and frightened. They may also be dreaming that their children will succeed where they have not, and be the means of fulfilment for some of their own hopes. As Yaconelli puts it:

> Maybe what's most unsettling about youth is the way in which
> they can remind [grown-ups of their] own adolescent heart.
> Young people can stir up forgotten dreams and evoke unmet

longings within adults. They can unearth the contradictions between the hopeful vision of our younger selves and the mediocre and muddled reality of our adult lives.[13]

Back in the temple when Jesus was a baby, Simeon said to his mother, " . . . a sword will pierce your own soul too." (v.35). Children open up their parents to the heights and depths of their inner lives, the joy and pain of love. Parents and adults can opt out of that rollercoaster ride, by becoming distant to their children. Children can take on parental anxiety and fears, and decide not to rock the boat. Growing up is a communal adventure which involves risk, uncertainty, and letting go. To venture forwards into the next stage of maturity means leaving something behind, and that can feel sad or scary.

This hit me in a surprising way when our middle child departed for her gap year in India. It wasn't a new experience—we'd already done the airport farewell with her older sister when she went off to Africa. So I felt comfortable with my role as the calm, experienced, reassuring father. However, setting off to the airport in the middle of a dark February night with snow falling around us, I found myself reacting very differently, as this poem I wrote records.

Stepping Out

I knew that we would get there—
although the headlights piercing the darkness
revealed wind-whipped snowflakes
        determined to push us back.
But it was not this storm that engulfed
        me on that surprising day.

I knew the moment was coming—
Yet I was not ready for the deep pain that
        would smother the farewell speech
and make this cool veteran of goodbyes so mute and helpless.

I was there to support her . . . fearless Becky
who would always laugh and leap before
    realizing that she was out of her depth.
I would catch her, steady her.

How wrong I was. She stood tall among her new colleagues
self-assured, sociable, and told me not to worry.
And now I was the child, bumbling, lost for words,
uncertain of the next step,
engulfed in tears I did not really understand,
knowing that it was me who was stepping
    out on an unknown journey
while she in some way had arrived.

I've reflected long and hard on my reaction that day and concluded that it was about several things. There was the bitter-sweet experience of seeing my "little girl" stepping out as a "grown-up", with all that mixture of pride and pain, fear and fulfilment which such a moment contains. It was also touching transition moments from my own past, and the times when I had had to step out with varying amounts of support and understanding. There was also something about saying goodbye to my child, by which I mean not just my daughter, but the child within me that she evoked, the child who had played and laughed with her and who I hoped would not be lost in the serious responsibilities of adulthood now that she was going. While I was glad that she had "grown up", I didn't want myself or her to stop being a child, not in a certain sense anyway.

It turns out that although there is only one chapter of the Bible dealing with Jesus' childhood years, there is a great deal of insight within it about the process of growing up. It is clearly something that happens in community—young and old are involved together. As such, it cannot just be contained in certain periods of life—adolescence, for example. It is a lifelong process, and one that at times will be painful and demanding. Furthermore, the journey is more paradoxical than simply from being a child to being an adult. It is something more like becoming a childlike adult, or a grown-up child. Those paradoxes emerge in Jesus and are linked with his relationship with God. His growing awareness of God as his Father points to the importance of taking our inner child into our adult life and maturity. This highlights the significance of an intergenerational church which, by the very interactions of children, young people, adults, and elders, ensures the gifts of these life stages all contribute to the wholeness of the community experience and to individual journeys to maturity. How, then, might we portray the idea of a "grown-up child"?

For further thought and discussion

- Share a "growing-up" story which illustrates something of the turbulence of adolescence.
- Read Luke 2:21–40. How were the needs of young and old met in this story? How possible is it to be an intergenerational church today, and how might it be more like that for you and/or your church?
- Read Luke 2:41–52. What insights does this story have for parents and children, and what can we learn from it about growing up?
- What makes growing up difficult, and how can we overcome those things?

CHAPTER 2

What is a grown-up child?

I've always enjoyed the story of the mother who shouted up to her son that it was time to go to church. When he insisted that he was not going, she asked for two good reasons. "I don't like the people and they don't like me," he replied, and asked in return for two good reasons from her. "Well, you're forty-nine years old," she replied, "and you're the vicar." I'm sure we have all encountered adults who, in varying degrees, have never stopped acting as children, while the reason I find it funny is that, as a vicar, I normally have to be seriously responsible. If that is one image we might have of a "grown-up child", the opposite is the child who acts grown-up before their time. We might recall the over-sensible Saffron in the sitcom *Absolutely Fabulous*, whose character is the flip side of her mother's irresponsibility.

Just as in literature it is often easier to create a loveable villain than a saint, it is difficult to devise images of maturity that are not responsibly dull or excitingly flawed. *Absolutely Fabulous* is a case in point. The famous female duo, Edina and Patsy, were described by Anthony Horowitz as "wonderful monsters who manage to encapsulate everything that is shallow and destructive in humanity while still being loveable".[14] The idea of "wonderful monsters" points up the huge paradox that terrible flaws might still attract and warm us to their humanity, and in certain ways build relationship. Yet living with them might be another matter altogether!

The story of the two sons

These sorts of paradox are there in Jesus' famous story of the two sons (Luke 15:11–32). The younger son is insensitively irresponsible. Asking his father for his share of the estate was effectively saying, "I wish you were dead." He has to learn the hard way that the freedoms he so craves are not automatically discovered in his leaving home. In fact, he finds that he is not free from his own spending compulsions—"he squandered his wealth in wild living"—nor the inhospitable conditions of the outside world—"a severe famine in that whole country"—nor the indifference of others to his plight—"no one gave him anything." He reaches the conclusion that he would be better off at home as a servant than in the misery of his current state. He is more right than he could possibly have imagined. His carefully prepared speech of remorse is swept aside in the lavish welcome and unrestrained delight of his father at his return. There is no lecture, no condemnation, no probationary period of acceptance, just a great party for a restored relationship.

This makes his brother very angry. He has been responsibly dutiful while his brother has been away. However, the homecoming and accompanying celebration expose a resentment that has clearly been festering. "All these years I've been slaving for you and never disobeyed your orders," he says to his father. He may not have been outwardly so selfish and insensitive as his brother, but clearly he has not enjoyed or appreciated his relationship with his father, who has to point out to him that, "you are always with me, and everything I have is yours." He is dismissive of "this son of yours"—not "my brother"—who has "squandered your property with prostitutes". (How did he know? Or was it his own repressed fantasies emerging?) We are left with a picture of a very unhappy, jealous, and frustrated character. And that's where the story ends. The huge paradox within it is that the lost son is found and the son who never went away is lost. The one who hoped he might be taken on as a slave finds himself celebrated as a son, while the one who has never stopped being a son is revealed as no more than a slave. Many of our concepts of responsibility and rightness are turned upside down.

Jesus is the master of telling stories that can shock us into seeing ourselves in new ways, and for our purpose in thinking about maturity there are a number of insights in this story. It is striking how little emphasis there is on the younger son's wrongdoing. The father accedes to his original request, and rejoices when he returns home. Maybe that suggests there was something right about his desire to enjoy life to the full, and the only problem was where he did it—on his own, in a far country, out of relationship with the father who loved him and gave him everything. You might say that the wild living did not need to stop—it was just that the best party was to be found at home. By contrast, the older son stayed at home but was unable to party. His life had become controlled, predictable, self-contained, and dull. Doing the right thing had become hard work and ultimately soul-destroying.

Such stories highlight the challenge of finding good images of maturity. We need something quite subtle to capture a virtue that is attractive and life-affirming. We need to negotiate the paradox that our efforts at goodness are only a short step away from pride and self-righteousness, while our mistakes and failings are only a short step away from grace and gratitude. Jesus seems to play with the idea of grown-up children. Indignant that the disciples were hindering the access of children to him, he said that the kingdom of God belonged to *such as* these, and entry depended on their ability to receive it like a little child (Mark 10:14–15). When the disciples were arguing about which of them was the greatest, Jesus placed a little child among them and said that to welcome a child was to welcome him, which was to welcome the one who sent him (Mark 9:37). At another time, Jesus denounced the people of the Galilean towns, where he had performed many miracles, because of their lack of response, contrasting them with the receptivity of children to the revelation of God (Matthew 11:25). What was it about children that he was affirming and encouraging the adults to imitate?

What is good in being a child?

William Wordsworth expresses the idea that as children we remain close to a pre-existent experience of God:

Our birth is but a sleep and a forgetting:
The Soul that rises with us, our life's Star,
Hath had elsewhere its setting,
And cometh from afar:
Not in entire forgetfulness,
And not in utter nakedness,
But trailing clouds of glory do we come
From God, who is our home:
Heaven lies about us in our infancy!
Shades of the prison-house begin to close
Upon the growing Boy . . . [15]

It is an evocative description that points to the instinctive spirituality of childhood as well as to the potential constrictions of growing up. Children can have a very real sense of God. However, the implication of a fading experience of God from childhood onwards has little biblical foundation nor echoes in modern understandings of faith development. In contrast to this and to those words of Jesus, the apostle Paul writes to the Corinthians of the importance of leaving childhood behind: "When I was a child, I talked like a child, I thought like a child, I reasoned like a child. When I became a man, I put the ways of childhood behind me." (1 Corinthians 13:11). And he encourages them to "stop thinking like children. In regard to evil be infants, but in your thinking be adults." (1 Corinthians 14:20). What is it about children that Jesus celebrates, and that Paul says we should leave behind? If Jesus is telling his disciples to be more like children, and Paul is telling the Corinthians to be more grown-up, is there a model of grown-up childhood that would satisfy both?

Children are being formed. As such they are dependent on others, open to explore, to question, to play, to wonder, to discover, to desire. The key to that is trust, trusting in the goodness of the world that makes experience and exploration safe and exciting, and trusting that disappointment can be negotiated with the help of those who will hold them and share it with them. If it is to be beneficent and carefree, then they need accompanying adults who walk with them. Unfortunately, if desires are not met and the pain of disappointment gets too great, the child says, "Enough". They survive by deadening their longings and suppressing their desires. Life's experiences start to be registered on a narrow emotional spectrum with limited highs or lows; they run away from sadness for fear that it will overwhelm them, and from joy for fear that it will let them down. They avoid the disturbance of creativity and guard the status quo. The energy of feeling is lost to them, as is the discernment that wells up not just from the intellect, but in the deeper intuitive places of the soul. As Simone Weil put it: "The danger is not lest the soul should doubt whether there is any bread, but lest, by a lie, it should persuade itself that it is not hungry."[16] They stop taking the risk of being children, of wondering and hoping and desiring.

Some years ago, I felt God challenge me in this area through an unusual experience. I was watching the women's tennis final at Wimbledon, and just as the match was coming to an exciting climax, I had to take my daughter to a party about ten minutes away in the car. I left with the match delicately poised at 5–5 in the final set and drove to the party and back. When I ran back into the house twenty minutes later, it was still 5–5 although almost immediately one player won the game and then the match. I was glad to see the ending but didn't realize the significance of the bit I'd missed until I began to hear the reports and read the papers next day. They were full of the twenty-minute game, the one game in the whole match that I had missed. "Perhaps the greatest game of them all" was the headline in one paper; "Twenty minutes that thrilled the world" said another—not just the centre court crowd, or the BBC television audience, but the whole world! "These two players enraptured the centre court on Saturday in what ranks amongst the greatest of matches. It will be remembered for 'the game' which one commentator encapsulated as 'a match within a match' . . . " And that was precisely the bit I'd missed!

I often find that such unusual coincidences beckon me to look closer and, like Moses with the burning bush, see if God wants to speak to me in some way through them. As I did that I sensed him saying: "You easily believe that, don't you? That you miss the best bits of life and have to settle for the second best; you're never quite in the right place, or doing the right thing." Just recognizing that seemed really important, because if that was my attitude, then it would easily be a self-fulfilling prophecy as I protected myself from the pain of hoping for too much. I could be shutting down the child in me with all his expectations and excitement, and not risking the heights. I could persuade myself that I was not hungry.

Jesus was not afraid to be a child in the sense of owning his needs, his incompleteness. "The Son can do nothing by himself; he can do only what he sees his Father doing." (John 5:19). His baptism becomes a powerful sign of this. His cousin John is amazed to see him there: "Do *you* come to me?" he asks (Matthew 3:14, my italics). He feels the incongruity of Jesus coming to a baptism of repentance. "Let it be so," answers Jesus: partly, I'm sure, because he wants to express his complete identification with humankind, but partly, too, to submit to ministry from the hands of another. Jesus does not act out an image of self-sufficiency, and he is amply rewarded as he emerges from the water and hears the voice from heaven: "You are my Son, whom I love; with you I am well pleased."(Mark 1:11). It is, of course, sheer grace, coming as it does right at the beginning of his public ministry. We could understand it coming after the temptations, or when he's been out in ministry for a bit and got some preaching and healing and deliverance under his belt. Then God might appropriately say "Well done, my boy, I'm really pleased with you—keep up the good work." Yet it's at this point, when he hasn't done anything, that the voice from heaven says, "You're my beloved Son."

These were foundational words for Jesus, and it's interesting that they are given again on the Mount of Transfiguration as he prepares to enter Jerusalem at the end of his life (Mark 9:7). He hears them just before his Galilean ministry, which would draw the crowds and witness spectacular healings and deliverance, and he hears them just before the final days in Jerusalem when he would be rejected and killed. The affirming fatherhood of God would seem to have been a key part of his negotiation of both heights and depths without disabling pride or fear.

The temptation to be falsely grown up

A deep awareness of being children of God enables us to live with the creative incompleteness of being a child, knowing that the world and we ourselves are in safe, loving hands. If—as adults—we suppress the child within us, then we can become falsely grown up and over-responsible. I have a card that I sometimes display which shows a man anxiously staring ahead, with the words: "Who'll take care of the world after I'm gone?" It is a weighty responsibility to assume.

In fact, this is very much how the foundational temptation of humankind is framed in Genesis. God is made out to be very restrictive and oppressive by the serpent: "Did God really say, 'You must not eat from any tree in the garden?'" Of course he didn't—all the trees that were pleasing to the eye and good for food were free to be eaten apart from just one, and the suggestion is properly countered by the woman. However, she has been softened up and falls for the counterpunch from the serpent about eating from the one tree. "You will not certainly die," the serpent said to the woman. "For God knows that when you eat from it your eyes will be opened, and you will be like God, knowing good and evil." (Genesis 3:1–5).

In one way the serpent is right: she does not die, not straightaway, but innocence has died, trust has died, an untroubled, carefree life has died, and the anxiety that has been sown—that God might not really want the best for them—has caused them to take matters into their own hands, and grab at what God wanted to give. We don't know what life without "the knowledge of good and evil" would look like, or how maturity would be expressed in such a condition. That goes beyond this story. What it does imply is that wanting the power that belongs to God and taking life into their own hands have entailed a deep loss, and their lives are now full of fear, guilt, blame, and mutual mistrust.

There are those who interpret this passage less as the great moral fall of traditional understanding, but rather as descriptive of the development of human responsibility. Marcus Borg talks of this story as depicting the birth of self-consciousness, or the separated self, which is a natural and unavoidable part of human development towards maturity.[17] Similarly, Dave Tomlinson suggests that the fruit had to be eaten as humanity outgrew paradise on the path to moral responsibility.[18]

Interestingly, Borg still retains the idea of it as a fall as well, a fall into self-centredness, estrangement, and exile. However, that is paradoxical because it is part of growing "up", and yet the term "fall" is a downward movement. It is hard to hold both ideas together. As a natural process it lessens the sense of moral culpability, but anticipates the need for further reconciliation and interdependence.

There is much in what they say that I want to agree with. It is true that the idea of "a fall" is less central to biblical theology than is sometimes presented in Christian teaching. Original sin can overshadow original goodness, even though the latter is at least as prominent a theme in the Genesis story, and looking forward to God's loving redemption is more important than dwelling on human sin and guilt. We have seen, for instance, how Jesus focuses not so much on the moral culpability of the younger son but more on his return and the restored relationship with his father. It is also true that moral boundaries have sometimes been simply means of control, and breaking them has been about growing up rather than just being rebellious.

I also think that the judgements announced after "the Fall" are as much a theological interpretation of life as it is experienced—where humans know good and evil, where childbirth can be painful and dangerous, where work can be hard and demanding, where relationships can be deceitful and oppressive, and where death is universal—as the arbitrary punishment of a God whose will had been crossed.

However, Tomlinson overstates his point when he suggests that life before the Fall was almost sub-human, with paradise as an indulgent life of pampered innocence until Eve courageously led her husband into the brave new world of moral demands and ethical decisions. This does violence to the actual story as it is written in Genesis. There is purposeful work and moral demand in the human world before the fruit is taken (Genesis 1:28, 2:15–16). There are grown-up responsibilities to be embraced. Beyond that we can only speculate what life would have been like.

For me, therefore, it is a story about being grown-up children, living with real freedoms and responsibility, and yet within the boundaries of a relationship with God. As with Jesus' story of the two sons, it implies that humans live best when in a right relationship with a generous and loving God.

As Walter Brueggemann puts it:

> The destiny of the human creation is to live in God's world,
> with God's other creatures, *on God's terms* . . . the *freedom* of
> human persons to enjoy and exploit life and the *vocation* of
> human persons to manage creation are set in the context of
> the *prohibition* of God . . . This text fixes the issue in terms of
> accepting the realities of our life with God. Our mistake is to
> pursue *autonomous* freedom. Freedom which does not discern
> the boundaries of human life leaves us anxious.[19]

That prohibition is not heavily restrictive, and like law elsewhere in the Bible is presented in terms of preserving rather than denying human freedom and fulfilment. There is, though, a clear implication that human enjoyment of the world, and the responsibility of management within it, happens when the right boundaries are understood, and particularly when God is allowed to be God. Working out the balance of human vocation and permission within the boundaries of God's rule is at the heart of being "grown-up children", but Genesis 3 describes real loss if we take life into our own hands and try to make ourselves God.

Taking life into our own hands is not just about getting hold of the material things we think we need. It is grabbing the creative knowledge that is God's and determining our own world and our own identity. Growing up can be very frightening as we emerge from the securities of childhood into a vast and complex world of new freedoms and possibilities, and it's easy to grasp at some off-the-peg identity to cope. I remember, for instance, the insecurities I felt on the eve of ordination. I was still young and clearly anxious about my new reverend persona, so I set out to project myself as simply a normal person. In fact, I actually wrote an introduction to myself in the local parish newspaper on these lines. There was a hit record at the time (it was the punk era) with the refrain, "Nice legs—shame about the face". So my article was headed, "Normal person—shame about the job". I can see now that part of me was so frightened by the expectations that might come with my new role that I needed to emphasize my so-called "normality" from the start. It took time for me to catch up with what God knew me to be when he managed to communicate his call on my life. I'd heard the call, but not yet integrated it into my conscious identity. God knew me better than I knew myself.

In my experience, God is both the open sea that carries us towards new worlds and new possibilities, and the anchor when the waters get rough and overwhelming. Without him we can end up with no clear sense of who we are, on the one hand endlessly tossed around by different possibilities, or on the other very firmly tied up in harbour. We easily create a world of no surprises, living firmly within perceived limitations, and with strong control and boundaries. Becoming more childlike is to enter the far more exciting (and sometimes scary) reality of God's world.

The importance of play

One way of perceiving this is through that important childhood activity of play. Play is about experimenting and exploring roles, relationships, and skills, and just enjoying things as an end in themselves rather than because they serve a purpose. Real play has a quality of self-forgetfulness in an encounter with the goodness of life. Jean-Jacques Suurmond imagines, from the creation stories, that God meant the world as a game. He notes how, in the account of creation, it is the Sabbath that is the climax, not the creation of human beings, and humankind is therefore first called into experiencing Sabbath where creation is celebrated, grace is enjoyed, and the goodness of God is recalled and expressed in worship. According to Suurmond, play takes us close to the character of God because God is not useful or serving a purpose, but is an end in himself. So play leads us beyond the world of work and necessity, achieving and usefulness, into the space of God's ultimate meaning:

> As priests of creation, human beings are called to live in a way that the rest of the world as yet cannot, so that the purpose of creation becomes clear. The lives of plants and animals are dominated by necessity and utility and directed towards the preservation of the species. However, the activities which most distinguish human beings from animals transcend this and have the free character of a game: worshipping, celebrating festivals, creating art, loving without an object or a reason. Animals have no festivals and create no art: they couple but do not love. The more human

beings learn to live playfully, the more human they become and
the more they begin to resemble God who has directed creation
towards the Sabbath game.[20]

Being a grown-up child

To live playfully is essentially childlike. It is to enjoy and express who we
are. It is to wonder and worship. There is, though, an important adult
component to this which is about integrating our experience with that of
others, and learning to give as well as receive. To do this means discerning
appropriate boundaries to human experience, being able to say "No" and
"Enough". This is much needed in a society which has dismantled many
of those boundaries and dedicated many of its prime resources of money
and talent to inflame desire and increase consumption. If economic
growth is the only end, and consumer spending is the engine for it, then
the temptation will be not just to manufacture goods to meet real human
needs, but to manufacture needs to buy the goods being produced. In his
book *Consumed*, Dr Benjamin Barber calls this the ethos of infantilization
that turns adult shoppers into impetuous and grasping teens, crying, "I
want, I want." The resultant society is increasingly indulgent, obese, and
insatiable.[21]

Ben Elton, in his book *Blind Faith*, paints a frightening picture of
a society where desire, emotion, and experience are left completely
unfettered. It is a post-apocalyptic scenario where space and privacy have
been obliterated by a combination of global warming, which has caused
the flooding of habitable land space, and "big brother" technology, which
means all human activity is recorded and shared. Science and reason
are part of the old discredited order; the gods of love and experience
are to be worshipped, so every emotion is indulged, and shared with
all. At work, where there are no official hierarchies in order to avoid
damaging people's self-esteem and making them feel uncomfortable,
people control the environment on the basis of being the loudest, most
shameless "emoter". Banners proclaim: "How do you feel? Tell someone
right now!" or "Sharing. What's not to like?" All this is undergirded by
a theology that makes human experience central in the name of God.

"'Man is God's work!', Confessor Bailey thundered to his congregation. 'Everything we are, everything we do, everything we say is the creation of the Lord and the Love. Therefore, when we talk about ourselves we are *actually* talking about God! Each thought we have, each word we say, each part of the bodies in which we exult is a gift from the Love and should be held up high for all to see!'"[22] Not surprisingly, disrespect of anyone else's experience was the big sin, with offence taken at the slightest hint of it.

It is a caricature, but like every good caricature exaggerates tendencies of our culture we might recognize. In a *Big Brother*, reality-TV, social-media world we are fascinated by watching the experience of others and draining the cup of experience to its dregs. In a celebrity culture, people are famous for being famous. Submission to a big story that defines truth bows before every person's opinion and experience as told in blogs or Twitter or in the pages of Wikipedia. While there is something good about the democratization of communication, the dangers of narcissism and dumbing down are real.

These trends are not all negative, and we would not just want to return to the tight-lipped, repressed, and deferential culture of the past. In the church we have rediscovered a warmth to our worship and an expectation of real encounter with God which is rich and wonderful. But there are warning signs as well. Our culture is full of undiscerning spirituality, and it can enter the church. There can be a running after the next big experience, with all the hype of signs and wonders. Not long ago I came across a leaflet that was advertising a period of 24/7 prayer on our local university campus. There was a series of belief statements on the front, such as "We believe in a God who loves to answer prayer . . . ". Most of them resembled familiar statements of faith, albeit with a more experiential tone. But one particularly caught my eye: "We believe that boredom is a sin," it asserted. I guess they were saying that not to be excited about living and serving in God's world revealed that you were lacking something. But when do we become dependent on the excitement rather than the God who lies behind it? I often used to say to those who led our more contemporary worship in church, when we received complaints about a dull service, that being bored is the only guarantee of disinterested worship—i.e. I'm here for God, not just myself! It was partly tongue-in-cheek, but underneath lay a serious point.

We are to be *grown-up* children—not to lose the positives of childlikeness but to balance them with grown-up attitudes, the most important of which will be the ability to contain, interpret, and transcend immediate experience by reflection, setting limits and boundaries, living with consideration for others, and handling complexity.

In *The Road Less Travelled*, Scott Peck stresses the importance of recognizing that life is difficult and identifies four tools of discipline by which we transcend difficulties creatively rather than just becoming victims. These are: the delaying of gratification, acceptance of responsibility, dedication to truth, and finally what he calls "balancing". By this last one he means bringing flexibility and judgment to bear on experience, to know our inclinations and feelings and desires but also to know when it is appropriate to express or act on them or not. So we need to have the courage to be completely real and honest, yet also the wisdom to know when withholding the truth is the most appropriate course of action. Similarly, we must be free to know and express our desires but also defer gratification of them when that is necessary for ourselves or others.[23]

I think he is describing something of what it means to be a grown-up child whereby we retain our ability to live in and experience the moment, to play, to access and express feeling, to welcome and embrace the new, but shaping that with the judgement and wisdom of reflection and sensitivity to others. It is claiming our identity, but also giving ourselves away for others. It is being innocent and wise, dependent and independent, free and responsible. In the next chapter we will think more about how this finds expression in our relationship with God.

For further thought and discussion

- Are you more likely to be called irresponsible or over-responsible, and why?
- Read Luke 15:11–32. In what ways does this story speak about God, sin, and growing up? (Cf. also Luke 15:1–2.) Which character do you identify with, and how does the story speak to you?
- What are the characteristics of children that Jesus wanted us to imitate?
- " . . . the idea of 'a fall' is much less central to biblical theology than is often presented in Christian teaching. Original sin overshadows original goodness, even though the latter is at least as prominent a theme in the Genesis story, and looking forward to God's loving redemption is more important than dwelling on human sin and guilt." Do you agree?
- What "grown-up" attitudes do you feel to be the most important for you, the church, and the world today?

CHAPTER 3

Living with God

Living with God has always been to some extent mysterious. David Hare's play *Racing Demon* takes a penetrating look at the Church of England. It opens with a cry from the heart of the Rev Lionel Espy who addresses God plaintively, bemoaning the fact that he never seems to say anything, especially when people are in a bad way and need something more than silence. While people understand that God is not just going to turn up in front of them, there is a perpetual absence, he suggests, that is getting him and others down. "God. Where are you?" is his cry.[24]

Some may be shocked by such clerical unbelief and attribute it to the despair of a burnt-out priest, while others may be relieved at such honesty. I suspect, though, that many will have experienced those feelings at some point. Yet Anglicans who follow Morning Prayer in *Common Worship* each day will also say, "As we rejoice in the gift of this new day, so may *the light of your presence*, O God, set our hearts on fire with love for you . . . " (my italics).[25] Which is our experience: "perpetual absence" or "the light of your presence"? Maybe it's not as clear-cut as that, which makes it hard to describe.

The presence and absence of God

Of course, we need to understand what we mean when we talk of the presence or absence of God. Is it a subjective feeling, or an observation from life, or when things do or don't happen in the way we want or pray for? Talking of presence and absence in relation to God is clearly a shorthand for a complex reality. However, it does speak in a broad way of God's involvement with the world, and in my experience churches have not always been very good at naming—let alone interpreting—the nature of this involvement. In some traditional churches the language of spiritual experience is completely absent, and God is a distant creator and moral enforcer who is not much more than a name in the liturgy. By contrast, in some EPC churches God is a best mate who usually "turns up" in a "time of worship", which is a period of singing devotional songs rather than the whole service. The possibility of God's perceived absence is not owned, and that is fertile ground for a growing unreality. There are some important questions. Is God always there, the problem lying with our capacity to notice him? Or can he be absent from us? Couldn't God have made his presence more obvious to us?

It is certainly true that God's presence in the world is not unambiguously self-evident. Our observation of the natural world, as well as human society, reveals beauty, order, and goodness but also ugliness, chaos, and evil. If God intervenes in his creation, it is subtle and understated rather than brash and immediately observable. Human life can ostensibly proceed without him, even if it can be argued that life would be very different in his absence.[26]

That ambiguity is echoed in the pages of the Bible. Of course, the great theme is of a God who has revealed himself in creation, history, and supremely in Jesus Christ, and who continues to reveal himself through his Spirit at work in the church and the world. References to him speaking abound, "through the prophets at many times and in various ways, but in these last days . . . by his Son" (Hebrews 1:1–2). Individuals encounter God, as Isaiah did: "I saw the Lord, high and exalted, seated on a throne" (Isaiah 6:1); Job: "My ears had heard of you but now my eyes have seen you." (Job 42:5); or Jacob: "Surely the Lord is in this place, and I was not aware of it."(Genesis 28:16). Moses will not contemplate leading the people out of Egypt unless God's presence accompanies them. He asks to see God's glory and is permitted to hide in a cleft in the rock while God's glory passes by, so he will only see his back, not his face, "for no one may see me and live." (Exodus 33:12–23). It seems that he can see where God has been, but not his full presence. Interestingly, elsewhere Moses is described as one to whom God spoke "face to face", in contrast to other prophets to whom he reveals himself in visions, dreams, and even riddles (Numbers 12:6–8). Both passages, however, contain the tension of revelation and mystery, clarity and ambiguity, perspicuity and puzzle that characterizes the scriptural God.

There is also a counter-theme of God's hiddenness. Many of the Psalms echo this theme: "Why, Lord, do you stand far off? Why do you hide yourself in times of trouble?", "How long will you hide your face from me?", "My God, I cry out by day, but you do not answer." While Isaiah protests, "Truly you are a God who hides himself." (Psalms 10:1, 13:1, 22:2, Isaiah 45:15). The apostle Paul can talk both of the God whose "invisible qualities—his eternal power and divine nature—have been clearly seen, being understood from what has been made," and also of the God "who lives in unapproachable light, whom no one has seen or can see." (Romans 1:20, 1 Timothy 6:16).

Just acknowledging that ambiguity is important if we are to do justice to the biblical revelation and human experience. Otherwise we easily create unreal expectations or trite certainties on the one hand, or a relational distance that amounts to a practical atheism on the other. Mystery is an appropriate word, as long as we think carefully about how we understand and approach that mystery as grown-up children who are ready to wonder and think at the same time. So how do we frame this ambiguous experience of God, both philosophically and theologically?

Understanding God's ambiguous presence

The sharp end of God's ambiguous presence in the world is the fact of evil. Some philosophies get round this by saying evil is essentially an illusion, but that does not seem true either to what goes on in the real world out there, or to the inward experiences we all have. So I want to acknowledge that there are plenty of bad things happening in the world which cause real pain and suffering, and their existence poses questions about God. Once owned as real, evil threatens to undermine the power or the goodness of a sovereign creator.

The question of why an omnipotent and infinitely good and loving creator has allowed the presence of evil in the world is real and troubling. It would appear that either he is not powerful enough to do anything about it, or he does not care enough. I suspect both of those are thoughts about God that we live with more than we realize. On the one hand, assuming God is not very powerful, we relegate him to the margins of life like some absentee landlord, or fall into a dualism that gives as much power to the forces of evil as to God. On the other hand, we can fear that God is unlovingly negligent or even some sort of tyrant. I remember well someone once writing to me about their image of God in these terms: "God is sovereign but impersonal. I see him as a being indifferent to my needs—unloving—just a wrathful entity in the sky whose main business is to make it tough for people in general and Christians in particular. He has much more important matters to deal with than me. I am insignificant, just part of the church to be refined into perfection." It is not often expressed as graphically as that, but some such thinking can be there even if never fully articulated or consciously owned. We will return to how we integrate our experiences of an evil world into our spiritual journey, but for now we need to stay with the philosophical question.

If we are not to conclude that God is either powerless or indifferent in the face of evil, then we need to have some other way of understanding his relationship with the world that explains the presence of evil without compromising his character. That is usually expressed in terms of the freedom he has given to men and women to enable an authentic personal relationship with himself. However, even talking about human free will is not completely straightforward, because freedom is never absolute or total but will be exercised within certain limits. It will be circumscribed by the nature of who we are and the experiences we have had. A fish is free to swim through the ocean, but not to live out of water on land. A bird can launch itself safely from the top of a tree, but if we were to try the same we would plunge fatally to the ground. Our nature determines our freedom. Moreover, as we are conscious human beings our freedom will be shaped not just by our inherited attributes but by nurture as well—the attitudes we have imbibed, the opportunities we have been granted, and the love we have received. Freedom is real but is relative, and reflects our nature and history.

In the light of that it could be suggested that a good God would have created beings that had freedom but were of a nature that would always choose the right. One day we imagine that we will dwell in God's presence and always choose to love and worship him without contradiction, in the mystery that we call heaven. So why is that sort of response not possible from the outset? Why could we not have had a nature that always responded to God rightly and so removed the possibility of evil from the world?

When my son was small, he had a habit of asking "why" questions. Although I tried to give answers within the limits of my knowledge and patience, inevitably when each one provoked a further "why" we eventually reached the point where I would bring things to an abrupt conclusion with a rather terse, "Well, it just is." For some we may be getting near to that point as we try to understand the particular freedom that we have been given by God. But for those who want to persevere, I think there is more that we can say.

Space for love

When Jonathan Sacks asks the question, "Why would a being independent of the universe wish to bring a universe into being?" he answers, "There is only one compelling answer: out of the selfless desire to make space for otherness that, for want of a better word, we call love."[27] The particular freedom that we have been given as human beings is not just to eat, or guard our territory, or do whatever we need to survive, but to love. When we reflect on the nature of love, then the measure of human freedom begins to take shape. We may not be helped by the great emphasis today on romantic love, a feeling that we can fall into and out of, and over which it can seem we have little control or choice. The biblical concept of love—"*agape*"—is very different, much more about an initiating response of goodwill, loyalty, and faithfulness to another. It is love in action. It cannot be expressed just through some instinctual choice or any sort of inevitability. A real measure of freedom and creativity is necessary for that sort of love.

Sacks talks of the freedom necessary for love in terms of a "space for otherness". This begins to give us a way of understanding the nature of God's presence in the world, which needs a certain sort of space to allow love to grow. God's presence needs to be neither coercive and overwhelming nor completely remote and unknowable. We might think that if only we saw more of God we would inevitably be attracted to him and respond with love and obedience. Yet as we have seen biblically, there is a strong hint that too much sight could be destructively overwhelming—you cannot see God and live. People who encounter God in the Bible are often profoundly shaken and disturbed (see, for example, Isaiah 6:5, Daniel 8:15–17, Luke 5:8, Hebrews 12:28–29, Revelation 1:17). The Post Communion prayer for the third Sunday after Trinity in the Anglican *Common Worship* expresses it well: "O God, whose beauty is beyond our imagining and whose power we cannot comprehend: show us your glory as far as we can grasp it, and shield us from knowing more than we can bear until we may look upon you without fear . . . "[28]

When Britain experienced a solar eclipse, dire warnings were issued about looking directly at the sun to observe the phenomenon. The light would be more than our eyes could safely endure. In the same way we can only know a *measure* of the reality of God if we are not to be blinded by the light of his holiness and moral purity. So in his love, God reveals himself in such a way that we can respond, and grow. He does not impose himself so as to violate our freedom, or hide himself to excuse our indifference. The right "intermediate space" is necessary for the otherness that love requires, so the possibility of the rejection of that love is credible but not inevitable, and does not undermine human responsibility or ultimately the loving goodness or power of God. The world will therefore need to be a place that both reveals God but also conceals him, in a way that is enough for us to respond to him without being overwhelmed or compelled.[29]

While it will never be easy to create a simple philosophical frame to understand the nature of God's presence in human life and resolve the dilemmas of God's sovereignty, human freedom, and the origin of evil, the idea of "a space for the otherness that we call love" feels experientially helpful, and orientates us towards the future rather than the past. Within that space, we have the freedom to grow and our journey through life becomes a maturing into the love of God. The nature and depth of our consciousness of God is shaped by the goal of enabling a real and growing relationship. This gives us a perspective on any sense of God's hiddenness or absence. If the language of personal relationship is to have any meaning, then there has to be a very real substance to this otherness.

Metropolitan Anthony Bloom expresses this so well in the context of writing on prayer:

> ... prayer is an encounter and a relationship, a relationship which is deep, and this relationship cannot be forced either on us or on God. The fact that God can make Himself present or can leave us with the sense of His absence is part of this live and real relationship. If we could mechanically draw Him into an encounter, force Him to meet us, simply because we have chosen this moment to meet Him, there would be no relationship and no encounter. We can do that with an image, with the imagination, or with the various idols we can put in front of us instead of God ... A relationship must begin and develop in mutual freedom.[30]

He then goes on gently to point out that we are a great deal more absent to God than he is to us!

Much of our sense of God's absence will be due to our lack of awareness, our failure to be attentive to his presence. This would account for the amount of language in the New Testament stressing the importance of "seeing", including the deeply ironic words of Jesus in the context of the parable of the sower, that "they may be ever seeing but never perceiving, and ever hearing but never understanding; otherwise they might turn and be forgiven!" (Mark 4:12). It seems that it is all too easy for us not to see or discern the hand of God in our human affairs.

Once I was driving home from leading a teaching morning in a church. It was lunchtime, and feeling rather hungry and knowing my wife was away, I was delighted to see a KFC by the roadside. I pulled in and put my hand in my pocket to find very little money, but there was, to my joy, a voucher that I had been given when buying some stuff at WHSmith a while before. I looked carefully at the small print to see if it was still in date, and to my delight found that it was. However, it did also say, "Not valid in any restaurant with a drive-through", which this one was. Did that mean "Not valid for use at the drive-through but maybe okay for eating in", or "Not valid in the restaurant at all if there was a drive-through", I wondered. I hoped it was the former because I was feeling really hungry now and only had enough money if the voucher was valid.

I felt it was rather an unfair condition. "I can only try," I thought, and marched in, presented the voucher, and asked whether they would accept it. The waitress only seemed to give it a brief glance before announcing immediately, "Sorry, I cannot accept it." I was half expecting it, but I still left disappointed at their seemingly arbitrary rules, and slightly puzzled that she could have noticed the small print so quickly and given her verdict. I was still bemoaning my bad luck to get so near but so far, when I looked at the voucher again. It was only then that I saw in big letters written across it, "McDonald's". I had got so wrapped up in the detail that I had missed the main message. In my embarrassment I imagined the waitress telling everybody for the rest of the day about the vicar who'd asked her if she would accept a McDonald's voucher for some KFC.

I am still amazed that I failed to see what was written so clearly on the voucher, but that is exactly what happened. And that is exactly what happens on a larger scale in life. We can get so absorbed in the practicalities of daily living that we just don't see the bigger picture, we fail to notice the signs of where we are and whose place it is. Yet when we begin to look at the world through the eyes of faith, and take time to become aware of God, I am also amazed at how often he *does* speak or how I *do* encounter his presence.

I am sure that much of the distance we feel from God is of our own making. However, sometimes it is of his. Many great spiritual travellers have described times of disorientation, when the outward forms of the spiritual life go dead on them, when prayer seems to yield no obvious fruit, or when inner convictions and consolations yield to confusion and disturbance. The Carmelites have written extensively of this, most notably St John of the Cross who termed it the "dark night of the soul".[31] If, sometimes, these are portrayed as the special experience of the advanced mystic, a modern Carmelite, Ruth Burrows, describes the dark nights as essentially the common lot, the ordinary trials which everyone must undergo and by which God purifies us.[32] What seems to happen is that the normal means of grace do not immediately yield results. In fact, nothing we can do moves us forward. We have to trust in spite of our circumstances and feelings.

In the end we are having to learn faith in God alone rather than any exterior or interior experiences he gives us. The consolations of faith are stripped away as it is purified even at the moment when it seems that it might be destroyed. We are learning detachment and patience.

We really are having to let God be God.

Presence and absence in the life of Jesus

Of course, Christians cannot talk about the presence or absence of God without referring to Jesus, "the image of the invisible God" (Colossians 1:15). Through depicting his character and teaching, his signs and wonders, and every way in which he did good, the Gospels substantiate the claim that "No one has ever seen God, but the one and only Son, who is himself God and is in the closest relationship with the Father, has made him known."(John 1:18). Nor is this revelation confined just to the short period of his earthly life and the written witness of the Gospels, foundational as they are. The scriptures envisage Jesus "appearing" in many situations. He was there in the Old Testament, so that when the apostle Paul writes of the Israelite exodus from Egypt, he says that "they drank from the spiritual rock that accompanied them, and that rock was Christ." (1 Corinthians 10:4). He continues to be present through the Spirit in the church which is described as his body (Matthew 28:20).

However, there was still mystery even in the days when he could be seen in the flesh. Often Jesus is heard requesting restraint or even silence from those he healed or delivered. His reticence could cause frustration, as when the Jews protest, "How long will you keep us in suspense? If you are the Messiah, tell us plainly." (John 10:24). At the resurrection itself, there is worship and doubt, and Jesus does not make himself known to the general population but only to those witnesses whom God had already chosen. "Blessed are those who have not seen and yet have believed," he says to Thomas (John 20:29). The essence of our relationship with God never ceases to be a matter of faith.

Shortly before his death, Jesus said something to his disciples that must have been deeply shocking. In essence he said that they were better off without him! (John 16:7). From then on, they were no longer to depend on his physical presence with them but on his Spirit working through them. What could be better than the actual company of Jesus? No doubt part of the answer was the potential of God's presence being released always and everywhere through the Spirit-filled church. In addition, though, there is something here of the disciples growing up, of entering the space created by the departure of Jesus and becoming—through the Spirit—more like God had made them to be, and doing the things for which he had called them. Again, maturity grows out of the right sort of space.

Perhaps even more shocking are the words Jesus cried from the cross: "My God, my God, why have you forsaken me?" (e.g. Matthew 27:48). Although they are taken from Psalm 22, they still remain a great mystery. Any interpretation of God's absence as of our own making becomes inappropriate in relation to Jesus. One line of understanding has been that the God whose "eyes are too pure to look on evil" (Habbakuk 1:13) has had to distance himself from Jesus at this point, as he carries the sins of the world. However, it is an interpretation that makes no theological sense to me, making the Father appear remote and squeamish, and rendering inexplicable the idea of God being *in Christ* reconciling the world to himself.[33]

Describing the relationship between God the Father and God the Son is always going to be full of mystery. Understanding it at this moment of huge and central theological significance is going to stretch our capacities of thought and language to the limit: "'Tis mystery all: the immortal dies! Who can explore His strange design?"[34] Many pictures and metaphors are needed to draw near to this mystery. If darkness came over the whole land as these events took place, what similar darkness descended on Jesus' soul? For me it was a perception of abandonment rather than active reality, yet still a horrifyingly real perception. The space for otherness had become filled with human evil as the love and grace of God were rejected and forces of destruction, hatred, and control took over. For that moment, Jesus encountered a complete absence of the intimacy that had characterized his life and ministry, of the love he had known from before the foundation of the world. Paradoxically, now for us that absence will never be the same again because it is the place where God in Christ is found. Now even when the "space for otherness" has become dark and frighteningly God-forsaken, it can be the place of encountering the most profound expression of God's love. I have witnessed in many pastoral situations the potential of Jesus to reveal himself as present within the darkness and wounds that many carry.

The writer to the Hebrews declares this of Jesus: "Son though he was, he learned obedience from what he suffered and, once made perfect, he became the source of eternal salvation for all who obey him . . . " (Hebrews 5:8–9). Here again is deep mystery. It seems to suggest that even for Jesus, the road of suffering—which, as we have seen, took him uniquely into a place of experiencing God's absence—became part of his perfection, which from a human point of view was clearly no static given, but was realized in the particular journey through this world that he took. For us too, then, it seems that living with God will be experienced as that particular combination of presence and absence, intimacy and distance, that will allow our growth to perfection in love.

The particular freedom that we have been given as human beings is as grown-up children, learning to love in the space that God gives us, which is neither coercive and overwhelming, nor abandoned and alone. Maybe in the end it is best expressed in a story:

A young North American boy had reached the age of manhood and was undergoing tests in preparation for his initiation rites, the last and most terrible of which was to go into the forest and spend a night alone. On the appointed night his father led him into the forest, collected a stack of wood, lit him a roaring fire and, instructing him to keep it going all night, went away promising to return first thing in the morning. All night long the lad huddled over the fire, shivering and trembling in fear, terrified of every snapping twig or bird cry that might signal the approach of a wild animal or demon. The ordeal seemed interminable, but finally darkness gave way to dawn and in the greyness the boy began to pick out the shapes of the tree trunks around him. Then he dimly discerned a tall, motionless figure standing under one of the trees. It was his father. He had been there all the time.[35]

For further thought and discussion

- In what ways do you experience God, and when has his presence been either particularly real or hard to discern?
- "The particular freedom that we have been given as human beings is not just to eat or guard our territory or do whatever we need to survive, but to love." Does that idea help make sense of the nature of God's presence in the world? Have you sometimes wished he could be more powerful or doubted that he cared?
- How does Jesus help us to understand or experience God? How do you understand his experience of abandonment on the cross?
- Have you ever felt overwhelmed by God, or abandoned by him?

CHAPTER 4

Providence and prayer

There can be few things more exciting than experiencing an answer to prayer. Suddenly God seems real, with a power that comes from beyond ourselves. I remember feeling that when I was weighing up a call to ordination. I knew something of my own heart, I had talked to lots of people and had encouraging responses, and I had even attended a selection conference and been accepted for training. However, in spite of all that I went through a questioning stage when I felt restless inside. I'd negotiated all these human processes, but was that sufficient to know the mind of God? Was I really sure that this was his will—indeed, had I really asked Him? So one morning I decided to pray. I realized that I could pray, "Lord, if it's wrong, please speak to me and show me . . . ", and that felt relatively safe, because if nothing happened then I could carry on as planned. Or I could pray, "Lord, if it's right, please speak to me and show me . . . ", and that was much harder because then something had to happen, God had to reveal his hand in some way. If nothing happened then I was faced with a complete change of direction. Lots of questions went through my head. Was it reasonable to ask such a direct prayer? How would he speak to me anyway? After much inner wrestling, I decided to pray the second prayer. Rightly or wrongly, I reasoned that this was the most important decision of my life, and if I was going to give myself into the service of God then he needed to be real, real enough to communicate. So, rather fearfully, I prayed the second prayer and, feeling more peaceful, turned to read the Bible passage set for the day in my notes. It was from Romans 10:

> How, then, can they call on the one they have not believed in?
> And how can they believe in the one of whom they have not

heard? And how can they hear without someone preaching to them? And how can anyone preach unless they are sent? As it is written: "How beautiful are the feet of those who bring good news!"[36]

The words leapt off the page at me and I was flooded with a deep assurance that God had heard my prayer and confirmed my call.

That moment was real and transformative. Yet the experience still raises questions. Seeking signs or testing God are not encouraged in the New Testament. "A wicked and adulterous generation asks for a sign!" said Jesus (Matthew 12:39). Yet there are numerous encouragements to pray, and to ask God for what we need. So how do we really understand prayer and providence? We have reflected on how the right sort of space is needed for us to respond to God in freedom and to grow up into the love for which we were created. In the light of that, in what ways can we talk of God "intervening" in human life without violating the freedoms that are necessary for love, or without acting arbitrarily or capriciously? Is there such a thing as a miracle? Does human maturity mean more or less of God?

Exploring interdependence

There is an old hymn called "Oh, the bitter shame and sorrow" with a line at the end of each verse designed to chart a growing maturity in the Christian believer, in terms of an increasing reliance on God. So it begins, "All of self, and none of thee", progresses to "Some of self, and some of thee", moves to "Less of self, and more of thee" before concluding "None of self, and all of thee!"[37] I guess that it is using "self" with a particular theological nuance, namely our sinful nature, that bit of us that acts self-centredly and even rebelliously towards God. In that sense, the displacement of self by God is to become more holy, more like him. That's fine—but it does depend on a fairly technical understanding of the words. It can suggest that maturity is about being more and more "taken over" by God and less and less "ourselves", more passive than active, more completely "dependent" on God. The implication can be that if only we got ourselves more out of the way and let God do everything, then all would be well.

Apart from needing to define more closely what God "doing everything" might mean, there is an immediate paradox here in that the human process of maturing appears the other way round. To mature humanly is to become less and less dependent on others and more your own person. On our human journey we start out as completely dependent on others for our very survival—physically and emotionally—and then embark on the road of growing independence. If we were to imagine that the phrases of the hymn related to our parents, then "None of self and all of thee" might apply to life in the womb or very early infancy, and "All of self and none of thee" would be much more like an adolescent or young adult. Interestingly, though, neither description feels like the finished article, and both the "none of self" state of dependence and the "none of thee" state of independence push us towards something further. That is the state of maturity which is an interdependence, able to be autonomous and access strength, but also rightly aware of personal limitations and the need of others.

There is a phrase attributed to St Augustine, "Without God we cannot, without us he will not", which seems to describe a spiritual interdependence that captures maturity more helpfully than "None of self, and all of thee". It points to a divine-human partnership as the way God chooses to work in the world. Part of this can be understood in very practical terms, as in these often quoted words:

> Christ has no body now on earth but yours; no hands but yours; no feet but yours. Yours are the eyes through which the compassion of Christ must look out on the world. Yours are the feet with which he is to go about doing good. Yours are the hands with which he is to bless His people.[38]

However, there is also here the mystery of faith and prayer. Mark records the extraordinary moment when Jesus returns to his home town and is faced with the contemptuous familiarity of friends and neighbours: "He could not do any miracles there . . . He was amazed at their lack of faith."

(Mark 6:5–6). This appears to be not just "without us he will not" but also to some extent "he cannot".

Prayer certainly takes us to the heart of the mystery of the divine-human partnership. How we pray will reflect how we understand God's power to intervene in the world. The traditional doctrine of God's providence encourages the belief that God is at work in the world, both in the big events of history and in individual lives. The instincts to thank God for good things, to ask for his help in times of need, and to trust him through difficulties, all betray some belief in providence. The model prayer that Jesus taught his disciples presupposes such belief: "Give us this day our daily bread"; "deliver us from evil"; "yours is the kingdom, the power and the glory". Many are the New Testament encouragements to ask for things in prayer: "Do not be anxious about anything," writes Paul to the Philippians, "but in every situation, by prayer and petition, with thanksgiving, present your requests to God." (Philippians 4:6).

The dilemmas of providence

However, it is also very obvious that believing in God's providence raises some very real dilemmas. If we believe that God intervenes in the world in response to our prayers, and we thank God when good things happen or when our prayers are answered, what happens to that belief when they are not answered, or God doesn't prevent some tragedy or evil? It is easy to be very selective in our application of providence and only see God's intervention when there is a good outcome. Furthermore, if we believe that God can cause things to happen directly, how does that fit with human freedom and responsibility? If we are asking God to overrule human freedom in order to make good things happen, where does he draw the line? Does he only overrule the decisions of bad people (however that is defined) or when they are making bad decisions? Once he starts overriding that freedom in some situations, why not always for the sake of a better world? However, if we say that he cannot do that because he values the freedom he has given us to grow in moral responsibility and love, then what becomes of our belief in providence? It is a real dilemma.

I remember once attending a very provocative service which was seeking to pose this dilemma in a stark way. We sang "All things bright and beautiful", which, on the whole, points us to the pleasanter side of creation ("the cold wind in the winter" notwithstanding), in order to draw out our gratitude and the ultimate affirmation that he "has made all things well". However, very soon afterwards we were asked to sing the Monty Python parody of this hymn. "All things bright and beautiful" became "all things dull and ugly", including the short and squat and the rude and nasty. The snake, the wasp, the hornet and the spikey urchin are all numbered within the Lord God's creativity along with the sick and cancerous, the foul and dangerous and the scabbed and ulcerous. The Lord God made the lot.[39]

The Pythons may be mischievous, but they pose the hard questions. The late David Jenkins did the same some years ago, as Bishop of Durham, when he questioned the empty tomb and the physical resurrection of Jesus. For him, the possibility of a miracle or even a resurrection that involved an empty tomb raised the spectre of a privileged few having access to the power of God, while big realities like Auschwitz or Hiroshima or the overcoming of famine were left to take their course.[40]

A providence that embraces darkness

These are real dilemmas, but it is noteworthy how parts of the Bible are willing to face them head on. In describing God's sovereign activity, they don't avoid the problem of the dark side of life, and are willing to see good and bad coming from the hand of God. In the second part of Isaiah, for instance, the prophet is robust in depicting the sovereign intervention of God in the world. He daringly describes the Persian emperor Cyrus as the Lord's anointed, whom he will use to subdue nations for the sake of Israel: "I summon you by name and bestow on you a title of honour, though you do not acknowledge me. I am the Lord, and there is no other; apart from me there is no God. I will strengthen you, though you have not acknowledged me . . . " He is saying that God has sovereignly chosen a pagan ruler to effect his purposes. He has even called him his anointed—his Messiah or Christ. Moreover, he is completely aware of the implications of such a declaration of sovereignty: "I form the light and create darkness, I bring prosperity and create disaster; I, the Lord, do all these things." (Isaiah 45:1–7). Maybe *Monty Python* is not so mischievous—the scriptures have got there long before. If God is sovereign, then even evil has to be part of his sovereign purpose. This is the big, broad-brush picture of God as Lord of history, whose good and loving purposes for his people will be achieved. A more detailed, nuanced picture of that victory will emerge in the New Testament through the death and resurrection of Jesus. But Isaiah's picture is still an important one for us.

Such a picture ensures that we do not slide into a dualism that makes evil as powerful as God. The Bible is clear that ultimate reality involves a God who is lovingly powerful and good. Evil is real, but contingent, a shadow rather than a substance, the absence of good rather than a force of its own. This can be an important pastoral insight. I have certainly found it helpful on occasions of heightened anxiety. In the summer of 1990 Saddam Hussein invaded Kuwait, and so began the whole train of events that led to the Gulf War the following January. I found the war deeply distressing, easily imagining it engulfing the whole Middle East and embroiling the world in a terrible conflict. For some weeks I lived with a paralysing anxiety. My son had just been born, and that probably added to my sense of vulnerability and my fears about the world we had brought him into. Then one day, as I was praying about this capacity to be disturbed by big world events, I sensed in my mind a call to read Isaiah 45. There I discovered the picture of the sovereign God who is Lord of history and who could use a pagan emperor for his purposes, and through whom even mighty Babylon (aptly situated in Iraq) had to submit to his will and purpose. It provided an anchor for faith in troubled times. It is by no means the complete picture, and a mature understanding of God will need to bring to it greater sophistication if the dilemmas of providence are not to undermine it. However, it certainly touched the anxious "child" within me at that time.

Such parts of the Bible encourage belief in God's active intervention in human affairs and leave him with the ultimate responsibility for good and bad. However, it may well be thought that talk of him creating darkness and disaster is fatal to any idea of a good providence. It certainly leaves a great deal in the realm of mystery, encouraging faith in the final overcoming of evil but with the potential of portraying God as severe and even cruel in the meantime. For this reason, some people are reticent about talking of God "intervening" in the world at all. It is only *people* who are seen as agents of intervention, and so when we pray it is we who change, and the outside world is changed through us. To claim more, they say, leaves God open to charges of capriciousness or of being the agent of evil.

The complexity of causality and "the experiential surplus"

Yet I believe that the idea of the divine-human partnership, or our interdependence with God, can bring a more sophisticated understanding of providence to these dilemmas. The starting point is the recognition of the complexity of causality, which is evident in the gap there often is between what we do and what actually happens. At the time of writing, parts of England are facing severe flooding. Various causes are put forward by the media or politicians, the Environment Agency, or the people who are on the receiving end. On the one hand it is simply about unprecedented amounts of rainfall, but on the other it is human negligence, a failure to dredge rivers or to invest in flood defences. The amount of rainfall could be an arbitrary freak occurrence, or the effect of global warming on our weather patterns. Almost certainly, none of these is the simple cause alone, but rather it is a combination of factors—some within human control, others not.

I would suggest that we all experience that mysterious complexity in what happens in our lives. We do something straightforward and simple, and it turns out to have unexpectedly good consequences: we revise for an exam and just the right questions come up; we email a friend and it turns out to have been just when they needed encouragement; we go to a party and meet someone who will change our lives. Equally, it may be the sense of being protected or spared from something: we oversleep and miss the train on the day of a crash; we fail an exam and end up on a different course which, with hindsight, is much more suited to us; we break a leg and in hospital a worse problem is discovered and treated.

The gap between what we do and what actually happens, between action and consequence, is what we might call "the experiential surplus". It is a universal experience which some will call chance and others God's providence. Richard Bauckham puts it like this:

> It is in this constant surplus of what happens beyond what we are able to achieve that we see the hand of God. Human freedom plays a part in what happens, but so does God's greater freedom. That is why what often makes people specially aware of providence is a specially remarkable coincidence. Coincidence brings home to us that what happens is not what we plan.
>
> But then we have only to think about it to realise that all of life involves coincidence. It is coincidence that weaves the threads of human actions into the tapestry of actual life. The more we realise this, the more we can see how God's providence is constantly making something worthwhile out of our own small contributions to life.[41]

The important point is that it is not one *or* the other: "Without God we cannot, without us he will not." Interdependence is the mark of maturity.

If interdependence is a helpful way of seeing our relationship with God, then for grown-up children there will be a blending of dependence and independence. We never cease to be dependent on God; no matter how clever we are, Jesus still encourages us to ask boldly and even to expect the extraordinary (see, for example, Mark 11:22–24). If we are to be childlike in the asking, then we will ask even if sometimes our motivation may be less than perfect and our understanding small. Children ask indiscriminately, and a good parent is able to say no (and yes) appropriately. When my children were young, as Christmas drew near the list of what they wanted began to grow. In fact, my son's favourite reading became the Argos catalogue, which he scanned at bedtime and then made his requests. Quite often they were completely inappropriate. When he asked for a Black and Decker power drill the answer had to be no. Yet as I reflected on some of the presents he wanted, I could see that really he was saying, "I want to be like you," "I want to do the things I see you doing." With a little imagination, gifts could be given that honoured the spirit of the request even if it could not be fulfilled to the letter. So even if the request had to be declined, the asking was still important, and built understanding and relationship.

Interventions and "miracles"

In prayer, the growing-up process will shape the way we ask. Our asking will come increasingly from a deepening relationship with Jesus: "If you remain in me and my words remain in you, ask whatever you wish, and it will be done for you." (John 15:7). Furthermore, there will be a changing relationship to the way we expect God to intervene and to the so-called miraculous. Some dismiss the latter, including a physical resurrection, because it raises too many problems of God's unfairness or arbitrariness. However, do we have to insist that if God is going to do anything he must do *everything*, at least everything we think he ought to do? Is that not potentially limiting God to our understanding and denying the mystery of providence?

We might expect there to be extraordinary manifestations of God in and through the person of Jesus Christ. Once we have conceded the incarnation, then miracles and resurrection are a perfectly reasonable consequence. Augustine, again, has put it well when he says of the miracle of the turning of water into wine at Cana:

> Our Lord's miracle in turning water into wine comes as no surprise to those who know that it is God who did it. At the wedding that day, he made wine in the six waterpots he had had filled with water; but he does the same thing every year in the vines. The servants put the water in the jugs, and he turned it into wine. In just the same way the Lord turns into wine the water that the clouds drop. Only that does not amaze us, because it happens every year ... So the Lord kept back certain unusual things for himself to do, to wake us up with miracles to worship him.[42]

There is so much in those few words. First, in pointing to the "miraculous" within the natural world, Augustine is helpfully undermining the false distinctions we can make between the "natural" and the "supernatural", and encouraging the discovery of God in all of life. Of course, there will be both "everyday" happenings and "certain unusual things", but God is not more in the one than the other. In fact, in the scriptures, so-called supernatural acts may be nothing to do with God at all. For instance, the Egyptian magicians and sorcerers repeat the acts of Moses and Aaron, and Jesus can say of those who in his name prophesy, drive out demons, and perform many miracles, "I never knew you. Away from me, you evildoers!" (Matthew 7:23). On the other hand, those using more ordinary human skills can do so in a divinely inspired way—so the craftsman Bezalel is "filled . . . with the Spirit of God . . . to make artistic designs for work in gold, silver and bronze, to cut and set stones, to work in wood, and to engage in all kinds of crafts" (Exodus 31:3–5). Similarly, Solomon is given by God the wisdom he needs to rule (1 Kings 3:9–12). So the categories of natural and supernatural, or usual and unusual, are not the most important thing—but rather the presence (or absence) of God's motivating power and purpose within things.

David Jenkins is not far from this thinking when he says, "He transforms the natural, not by making it arbitrarily supernatural and so unnatural, but by enabling the unbelievable fullness of what is natural through unity with the unbelievably gracious divine."[43] "The unbelievable fullness of what is natural" may not be quite as strong as Augustine's "unusual things" that Jesus did "to wake us up with miracles to worship him", but both maintain a strong link between divine action and the natural world, encouraging the perception of God's action in ordinary life. Furthermore, the link between the natural and the "gracious divine" is focused, for the Christian, in the person of Jesus Christ. Here the divine-human partnership is a person; the "fullness" of human nature is revealed through unity with the incarnate Son of God. The incarnation is the seed of the new humanity which now bursts with transforming, divine potential. No wonder the presence of Christ on earth brings about "unusual things", but not so unusual that they are unrelated to the more ordinary life of the natural world and human experience.

Many of these distinctions boil down to our cultural expectations and definitions of the "normal". For a long time, our expectations in the West have been shaped by the rationalistic world view of the Enlightenment, with its closed system of observable cause and effect. Certainly, the scientific method has brought us huge understanding of the workings of the universe, from the macro-world of astrophysics to the micro-world of sub-atomic particles. As we enter the new worlds of artificial intelligence or genetic engineering, it is easy to conclude that science is conquering the territory that was once the preserve of God alone. If God is simply filling the gaps of human knowledge, then he will always be a diminishing reality. Yesterday's miracles become today's scientific orthodoxy.

Yet we have also observed how causality can be complex. Something may not always be explained by just one thing. It can be a false reductionism that asserts something to be "nothing but this" or "nothing but that". Reality is complex, especially if we are considering not just, say, the workings of a machine, but beauty or music or love. Moreover, the "experiential surplus" that is so characteristic of human life is more than a cerebral "God of the gaps" phenomenon, but a very real experience of serendipity, of life delivering more than we can explain or expect. That mystery can be interpreted either as chance, or as God's active providence, and such interpretation is a matter of faith either way. God's grown-up children will want to interpret it with a reasoned wonder.

As we have seen, Augustine links miracles with wonder. Their purpose is to evoke worship, not by transcending the natural order but by magnifying it to reveal God's providential action. The expression "signs and wonders" is therefore more helpful than "miracles" because it highlights their purpose—to awaken us to the beauty and creative goodness and power of God in all things. It is important that we try to understand providence and have a concept of the divine-human partnership if we are not going to make God a magician, and fall into a childish supernaturalism. Yet it is also important not to lose our sense of wonder, and simply imagine that it is human activity that is all-important and that God's part is no more than giving us instructions to follow. We are grown-up *children* who must never stop looking for the clues of God's active presence in the world and in our lives, and—when we find them—must express and confirm our delight in worship and gratitude.

Having said that, there is a spirituality that sees experiencing the supernatural as the mark of maturity, and miracles as the evidence of getting it right. Pentecostals have seen supernatural phenomena such as speaking in tongues as evidence of the presence of the Holy Spirit in a believer. Similarly, an attested miracle (or two) is one of the qualifications in the Roman Catholic Church for sainthood. However, it is hard to discover such an understanding in scripture. Jesus' own life is a case in point. Recorded miracles are common as he establishes his identity through his early Galilean ministry and proclaims the coming of the kingdom in word and deed. However, there is a pivotal moment when he begins the journey to Jerusalem, turning his face towards rejection, suffering, and death. A different, deeper transformation of human life is at work as he walks the path of sacrificial love towards the cross. Attempts to dissuade him from this are strongly dismissed, as Peter found, and the taunts of his enemies to call on some supernatural way to come down from the cross are ignored. There will be no providential intervention that spares Jesus from suffering and death, and followers are invited to walk the way of the cross too, and to find within it the way of life and peace.

I remember a churchwarden once telling me about the healing ministry in his church. "The most dramatic acts of healing", he said, "seem to be for those who are new to the faith or even still seeking. Sometimes more established believers see fewer outward signs." It is a useful corrective to the "Miracles are a sign of maturity" line of thinking. Maybe God does grant special signs of his grace to those who are being established in their faith and experience of God. It is when we are on an unfamiliar journey that we are most in need of signs. On a well-known route we may not even notice that they are there. The apostle John suggests as much when, at the end of his Gospel, he outlines his purpose in writing: "Jesus performed many other signs in the presence of his disciples, which are not recorded in this book. But these are written that you may believe that Jesus is the Messiah, the Son of God, and that by believing you may have life in his name." (John 20:30–31). The signs were there to evoke faith. Yet just before this, John has recorded Jesus' words to Thomas: "Because you have seen me, you have believed; blessed are those who have not seen and yet have believed." (John 20:29). The implication is that a maturing faith will be less dependent on signs and be able to trust God without visible or special evidence, seeing his transformative power at work in the outworking of more ordinary human relationships and actions.

Of course, to some extent we never stop being beginners in faith and in need of signs of reassurance. The Gospels present the miracles of Jesus as very much the overflow of his compassion, and it is good to encounter signs of his love carved deeply into the fabric of life. God is at work in all things, and equally he involves us in effecting his purposes. There is no dichotomy between believing in providence and acting responsibly. We pray, and we take action. Without God we cannot. Without us he will not.

For further thought and discussion

- As you read this chapter, note anything that excites you, or puzzles you. You might want to mark these with a "☺" or a "?" or a "!". Talk about your responses.
- Share a story which you interpret as an answer to prayer.
- "Without God we cannot, without us he will not." In what ways do you think that is true?
- How can belief in God's providence be squared with human freedom and responsibility?
- Does believing in "miracles" simply betray our lack of scientific understanding?
- How does this chapter contribute to your picture of human maturity?

CHAPTER 5

The mystery and mercy of suffering

We have explored the need for an appropriate space between us and God, to allow for a relationship of love. For love to grow, that space has to contain a real measure of freedom, allowing the possibility of love to be embraced or rejected. We have seen how human freedom interacts with God's freedom in the mysteries of prayer and providence. However, that freedom also allows the possibility of evil to spoil human life with all the pain and suffering that can ensue. We may be able to affirm the big picture of God's sovereignty in human affairs, and have a satisfactory philosophy of evil, but at some point it becomes personal. We are hurt, we are wounded, we suffer as a result of human sin and evil. Here we are entering sensitive territory. We need to *think* about suffering, but those who suffer need more than just thought. I can understand why C. S. Lewis introduced his book *The Problem of Pain* with the words, " . . . nor have I anything to offer my readers except my conviction that when pain is to be borne, a little courage helps more than much knowledge, a little human sympathy more than much courage, and the least tincture of the love of God more than all."[44]

How do we understand suffering?

As Job found out, well-meaning thoughts about suffering are of limited value when you are in the thick of it. However, that thinking needs to be done, not least because the reality of pain and suffering is one of the biggest stumbling blocks, for many, to an active faith today. It has not always been so. Alister McGrath reckons that it is only since the seventeenth century, when Christian apologists turned to philosophy to construct their defence of the faith, that suffering became so much of a problem for Christian belief.[45] Before that time, suffering and pain were much more integrated into a Christian vision of life. This is very evident, for instance, in the tone of the service for the Visitation of the Sick in the 1662 *Book of Common Prayer*, where it is robustly asserted:

> Wherefore, whatsoever your sickness is, know you certainly, that it is God's visitation. And for what cause soever this sickness is sent unto you; whether it be to try your patience for the example of others, and that your faith may be found in the day of the Lord laudable, glorious, and honourable, to the increase of glory and endless felicity; or else it be sent unto you to correct and amend in you whatsoever doth offend the eyes of your heavenly Father; know you certainly, that if you truly repent of your sins, and bear your sickness patiently, trusting in God's mercy, for his dear Son Jesus Christ's sake, and render unto him humble thanks for his fatherly visitation, submitting yourself wholly unto his will, it shall turn to your profit, and help you forward in the right way that leadeth unto everlasting life.[46]

I am not commending the tone of the Prayer Book, and certainly to our modern ears it seems heartless to see sickness as God's "fatherly visitation". God may use sickness, and reveal power in weakness (as the apostle Paul believed in relation to his thorn in the flesh), but sending it feels uncaringly proactive. Yet that toughness appears sometimes in the scriptures. The writer to the Hebrews invites readers to see hardship as the discipline that goes with being God's children. Hardship, far from being a stumbling block to the idea of a good God, becomes part of the assurance of his active care. "For what children are not disciplined by their father? If you are not disciplined—and everyone undergoes discipline—then you are not legitimate, not true sons and daughters at all." (Hebrews 12:7–8). It is not a line of reasoning that is commonly heard today. What has brought about such a change in perspective?

Clearly advances in medicine and technology have extended life expectancy, so we can more easily postpone thinking about eternity and our preparation for it, which is so much the thrust of the Prayer Book.

Moreover, when pain (at least in a certain sense) can be so effectively relieved by the palliatives of the modern world, it can seem much more of an alien intrusion into life, making any sense of it being introduced by a fatherly God all the more baffling. It can make God seem rather inadequate compared to the wizards of modern science. When pain wracks our bodies, or distress fills our hearts, we make our way quickly to the doctor or the counsellor.

Of course, this contrast can be overstated. It is only true in some senses that our modern age has relieved people from suffering. In the UK today, approximately one in four people will experience some kind of mental health problem in the course of a year, and in England one in six people report experiencing a common mental health problem (such as anxiety and depression) in any given week.[47] While these figures have not got worse in recent years, it appears that people cope less well with such issues, as the numbers of people who commit self-harm or have suicidal thoughts are increasing. Our life expectancy may have lengthened, our cures and control of physical pain improved, but our sense of well-being has not always kept up.

More significantly, though, the scriptures do not just encourage the passive acceptance of suffering as part of God's discipline. This more severe picture must be balanced with the Gospel portrayal of Jesus, who again and again healed people out of sheer compassion. In fact, indignation is sometimes a more appropriate description of his response to pain. Faced with the leper who begged him, "If you are willing, you can make me clean," some manuscripts describe Jesus' response as "filled with compassion", but other early manuscripts suggest he was "filled with anger" or "indignation" before he healed him (Mark 1:40–41). Again, as he witnessed the grief of Lazarus' family and friends, Jesus is recorded as being "deeply moved in spirit and troubled" before he went on to raise Lazarus from death. The word used speaks as much of anger and outrage as anything else (John 11:33). Jesus took up the fight against pain and suffering as much as passively accepting it.

Suffering and purpose

The alleviation of human suffering of every form should rightly occupy our best energies, and even if it can be shown to have some purpose and beneficial outcome, it is important not to romanticize it or take on a masochistic outlook. As one who has identified a certain "Unless-it-hurts-it-cannot-be-doing-you-good" inner script, I am conscious of the dangers of simply rationalizing a rather cruel approach to life. Slightly better is the "no-gain-without-pain" slogan, which is often used today in an attempt to engender discipline in a highly indulgent culture. I suspect, though, that it too has its limits as a motivating or comforting power, beyond fairly minor inconveniences. Nonetheless, it highlights the fact that the context of pain and suffering greatly affects our capacity to endure it. If we are conscious of the gain, then the pain is better embraced. The athlete training for the Olympics, the woman in labour, even the overweight person trying to diet endures hardships in this context.

It is also easy to see that there are many other contexts where pain is a friend, not an enemy. If fire did not instantly hurt us, then we would be in grave danger of being badly burned. If we did not feel unwell, then we might never get an illness diagnosed and treated. The question is whether such thinking can stand up to more overwhelming and debilitating forms of suffering. If it is true that suffering and pain are here to stay, that they are woven in some measure into the very fabric of life, then some understanding of them would seem to be one of the keys to enduring them.

This was the great insight of Viktor Frankl, survivor of three horrendous years in concentration camps during the Second World War, who could yet conclude, "There is nothing in the world, I venture to say, that would so effectively help one to survive even the worst conditions as the knowledge that there is a meaning in one's life. There is much wisdom in the words of Nietzsche: 'He who has a *why* to live for can bear almost any *how*.'"[48] Having something to live for which enables the endurance of suffering, and which even gives some meaning to it, became for Frankl a key therapeutic insight. He pioneered the school of psychotherapy called "logotherapy", which centres on the human search for meaning both in a general, existential way, and in a person's individual circumstances. His experience in the concentration camps and in his therapeutic practice was that the person with a recognized reason to live was much more likely to endure the hardships and challenges to life. Life needed some framework of meaning around it, which could be found in something we do, or in a relationship or other encounter, or in the attitude taken to some avoidable suffering.

Something of this was brought home to me when visiting a new Emmaus community that had opened in my archdeaconry. Impressed by their vision of addressing homelessness, I discovered more about their origins.[49] The first Emmaus community was founded in Paris in 1949, by an MP and Catholic priest known as Abbé Pierre who was concerned to provide homes for those who lived on the streets of Paris:

> One night, a man called Georges was brought to Abbé Pierre after a failed suicide attempt. Georges had been released after twenty years in prison, only to find his family unable to cope with his return home, leaving him with nowhere to go. He turned to the Abbé for help, but instead Abbé Pierre asked Georges to help him, building houses for the homeless mothers who came looking for his support.
>
> Georges became the first Emmaus companion, living with Abbé Pierre and helping him to build temporary homes for those in need, first in the priest's own garden, then wherever land could be bought or scrounged. He later said: "Whatever else he might have given me—money, home, somewhere to work—I'd have still tried to kill myself again. What I was missing, and what he offered, was something to live for."

Alleviating his suffering was not just about taking away the problem, but restoring a meaning to life.

As we have already seen, understandings of suffering have changed considerably over the years, and although we might find it hard to identify with the meaning given to it in the *Book of Common Prayer*, at least it was a meaning, and a very comprehensive one at that. Today, in many ways, we have compounded the problem of pain and suffering by losing any sense of its meaning. Because it feels much more of an alien intrusion into a world that prizes youth and celebrity, achievement and success, experiencing any unhappiness leads to a double burden: this is not normal, this is not how it should be.

The pursuit of happiness or "shaping for love"

Today's norms have been heavily influenced by an American culture founded on the "self-evident truths" of the Declaration of Independence, namely that our Creator has endowed us with the inalienable rights of "life, liberty and the pursuit of happiness". While the right to pursue happiness can appear reasonable and benign, it can easily be contracted to "the right to happiness" as if it is something life owes us. However, the discovery of happiness may be more paradoxical than that. In the same way that Jesus said the carefree life comes when we seek first the kingdom of God, so happiness is not necessarily gained by direct pursuit—it is the product of something else. We are happy when we have reasons to be happy, when we experience and enjoy that which gives life meaning rather than just pleasure. Describing the pursuit of happiness as an inalienable right all too easily leads to the individualistic and hedonistic culture that many contemporary societies now demonstrate. It raises expectations of a trouble-free life, of seeking individual fulfilment, and of avoiding pain at all costs. Perhaps that is why Scott Peck resonated so strongly with his American readers when he began his bestselling book *The Road Less Traveled* with the counter-cultural message that life is difficult.[50]

Some years ago, I contracted a mystery illness that laid me low for several weeks and seemed to elude diagnosis by the doctor. When I scanned the medical dictionary (it was pre-Internet!), I could imagine that I had everything apart from morning sickness. I felt tired and low and spiritually confused. Many prayers, including the laying on of hands by the church pastoral elders, seemed to have no effect. One morning I came across a line in the book I was reading, by Metropolitan Anthony: "So often what we would like to have through prayer, through the deep relationship with God which we long for, is simply another period of happiness; we are not prepared to sell all that we have in order to buy the pearl of great price."[51] The words penetrated my state of mind sharply. I just wanted to get better. I just wanted to feel happy again. I just wanted life to return to normal. But I began to see that God had a bigger, deeper, fuller agenda than just a return of happiness. There were lessons to learn in the vulnerability that my illness had created.

The pursuit of happiness can become self-serving, whereas faith puts a very different framework around suffering in seeing the meaning of life as love, and in particular the love of God. God has created the universe to make the space for the otherness that we call love. "Life is only for love, and time that we might find God"—words attributed to Bernard of Clairvaux on a prayer card that I have. If all experience is judged by this yardstick, then it takes on a very different meaning. Suffering can become part of how God shapes us to receive and give love. Certainly that is how the apostle Paul came to see it:

> . . . we also rejoice in our sufferings, because we know that suffering produces perseverance; perseverance, character; and character, hope. And hope does not disappoint us, because God's love has been poured out into our hearts through the Holy Spirit, who has been given to us.
>
> *Romans 5:3–5*

In the hands of a loving God, suffering can become part of the shaping of our character for love.

Of course, in choosing the word "love", we have to acknowledge that it can be a slippery word, used in many different ways. Every parent knows the fine line between love that is kind, protective, and encouraging, and love that is sentimental, indulgent, and always rescuing rather than fostering responsibility. Even our indulgent culture has recognized the concept and importance of "tough love", and that an easy happiness is not necessarily the most loving aspiration for another. However tough, being shaped for love is a powerful framework for understanding our suffering in the context of a God who defines love, neither as a rescuer, nor a nagging disciplinarian, but as one who cares enough to expect much from us.

Having the framework of tough love with which to understand suffering is a start, and sometimes we need that robust perspective to shake us up from the self-pity that can descend in hard times. Escapism, distraction, the flight into addictive behaviour or substances all too easily constitute our response to difficulty today. Embracing our circumstances, by faith if necessary, trusting in the love of God, taking up the battle against self-pity, are much harder. We certainly need the help of others to do this, and our vulnerabilities can be a way of pricking the bubble of our self-sufficiency. Many are the biblical exhortations to wait patiently for God—the return of peace or joy is not ours to command—but having a pastoral companion to wait with us can also be hugely important. In the Book of Job, Job's companions sat on the ground with him for seven days and seven nights without saying a word, because they recognized the extent of his suffering, and this was what he really needed rather than the torrents of words that followed. We may be able to take action against circumstances which cause suffering, but we cannot take people's pain away or lift the heaviness that can engulf them—the response to those circumstances is theirs. What we *can* do is wait with them until peace and hope return.

Job's so-called comforters were at their best when they spoke the least, a fact I am well aware of as I write this chapter! For all that we search for the meaning of suffering, the most important thing we can do for another is to stay with them rather than try to explain. Otherwise we almost invariably sound glib. Suffering is a deep, visceral experience which has the power to traumatize and bring our normal coping mechanisms crashing down. Abstract rationalization is not what we are looking for when we are wracked with pain. I remember well the spouse of a church leader who was going through some particularly hard family issues saying how difficult she found the number of well-meaning church people who sought to encourage her with verses like Romans 8:28 (" . . . we know that in all things God works for the good of those who love him . . . "). She did not feel that at the time, and however true the assertion, it only served to compound her pain, with a further element of guilt thrown in.

Those who accompany others in pain are all too aware of the depths of anguish that people bear. However, they will also know the resilience of the human spirit to survive, and even conquer. If suffering is woven into life, so is resurrection, the new life that constantly emerges from darkness. I have certainly experienced that sense of being more fully alive and creative after a time of pain or difficulty. This is the mystery of suffering. It must not be romanticized, yet it can contain a strange power to transform when experienced in the context of love, empathy, and care. I know that merely to say this runs the risk of some people thinking, "What does he really know about suffering anyway? Has he endured what I am facing?", to which the answer will be almost certainly not. In fact, sometimes I look at what other people suffer and find it difficult to imagine how I would possibly cope in such circumstances. As I watch the horrifying destruction in Syria or Yemen, the cruel persecution of Christians in some parts of the world, or even the frightening restrictions of age or dementia for many closer to home, I can wonder if my sanity—let alone faith—would stand up to the ordeal.

Living our own story

The point has to be that we cannot go very far with comparisons. In the end, we can only live our own story. Pain is subjective anyway. What one person can brush off as nothing will deeply affect another. What someone can endure at one moment, or in one situation, may be completely traumatic in another. In the C. S. Lewis Narnia story *The Horse and His Boy*, the characters encounter various lions on their journey, who are sometimes reassuring, sometimes frightening, sometimes protecting, sometimes seeming to fight and wound them. Near the end they encounter a lion for a final time, who turns out to be Aslan, who—to their surprise—identifies all the lions they have encountered as himself. As they have all had different experiences, they want to understand not only their own, but also those of others who have faced particular difficulties and hard encounters on the journey. But Aslan will have none of it. Several times he has to interrupt and say, "Child . . . I am telling you your story . . . No one is told any story but their own."[52]

Comparisons with others are rarely helpful. They can either make us hard and proud, like the Pharisee in Jesus' parable who thanked God that he was not like other men, or miserable and feeling hard done by, like the older son when his father threw a party to welcome back his returning younger brother. There will always be deserving poor who can make us feel guilty about how we use our time and resources, or the rich and comfortable who make us jealous of their seemingly easy passage through life. Unless we live our own story before God, we will never understand or experience anything of his ways. I found myself learning this once when I was on an individually guided retreat. I had been given Isaiah 43 to meditate on, and went back to my room feeling a bit disappointed. I knew all too well its heart-warming encouragements not to be afraid, and its promises of God's presence and protection through difficulties, and wondered how I could mine anything new from these all too familiar verses. However, sitting down to read I quickly reached beyond the oft-quoted bits to verses three and four:

> For I am the Lord your God, the Holy One of Israel, your Saviour;
> I give Egypt for your ransom, Cush and Seba in your stead. Since
> you are precious and honoured in my sight, and because I love
> you, I will give people in exchange for you, nations in exchange
> for your life.

My first reaction was, "That's a bit unfair. What about those other nations? Don't you love them as well?" For a good while I felt really angry and certainly could not appreciate God's redeeming and nurturing love for Israel, couched in terms that seemed to be at the expense of others. My reaction blocked any encouragement I might hear for myself. Then after some time of real wrestling, I felt I started to hear God's word to me. It began a bit like the words of Aslan: "I am not speaking to you about others. Their story is between them and me. I just want you to know that there is no one more important to me than you." I quickly knew that this was striking a deep note inside me. I realized afresh the extent to which I lived with an expectation that everyone else came first, or that they were more important. Perhaps it came from being the youngest in the family—I don't know. However, suddenly the anger was gone and all I knew was that this was God saying the opposite of that deep script within me. An overflowing joy bubbled up, and for several days I thought I was going to burst with that sense of his love. Each of us has to carry the particular vulnerabilities which God allows to affect us, and we have to live and understand and find peace within that story. There is no point measuring it against others, or trying to work out their story—not in general, anyway. Our concern must be to live out our own with gratitude and generosity.

Living in the now, trusting for the future

There are two further perspectives on suffering given to us by the scriptures which I have found helpful over the years, and both concern time. They could appear contradictory but are in fact, I believe, complementary. The first is about living in the present, in the now. Jesus tells us not to worry about the future—the future will take care of itself. "Each day has enough trouble of its own," he says (Matthew 6:34). I believe that God has been very merciful in building rhythms into time—day and night, work and Sabbath rest, seasons of the year. Sometimes we just have to take a day at a time. Sometimes even that may be too long and we'll need to concentrate on shorter intervals.

The book and film *Touching the Void* tell the remarkable story of how Joe Simpson escaped alone off the 21,000-foot Siula Grande in the Peruvian Andes, after breaking his leg and being left by his companion deep in a crevasse, presumed dead. Not only did he have to get out of the crevasse and make his way down the mountain with a shattered leg, but the clock was ticking as his friends would soon pack up the base camp and go on without him. His survival technique was to focus just on the next thirty minutes and to get down the mountain in half-hour chunks. Living in the very immediate present in the end enabled his survival. I remember that when our children were young, and parenting was demanding, the phrase "It's only a phase" helped us through. If it was a good phase, then we enjoyed it while it lasted. If it was hard, we reminded ourselves it wouldn't last forever!

Jesus encourages us to live in the now and not to worry about the future. There is down-to-earth good sense in this, as the famous quote from Winston Churchill illustrates: "When I look back on all these worries, I remember the story of the old man who said on his deathbed that he had had a lot of trouble in his life, most of which had never happened."[53] Much better to live one day at a time and to let the future unfold as it will. What helps us to do that is the second time-perspective which the scriptures encourage us to have—an eternal hope. "I consider that our present sufferings are not worth comparing with the glory that will be revealed in us," writes the apostle Paul to the Romans (Romans 8:18). We are back in the world-view of the *Book of Common Prayer*, where preparation for eternity is much more important than present trouble. However much life has been extended, and pain controlled, death will come—and the drama of our life will be but a short word on the great stage of eternity. The meaning of our life will be tested not by the wealth we have accumulated, or the successes we have achieved, nor even just by the impact our life and work will have made for future generations (the so-called legacy we leave, which has become such a contemporary concern). Christian hope imagines a future so much larger than anything contained by this life alone, and the bridge to it will be love. Without love we have nothing to take into eternity. Love is the lens through which the pain of our lives finds meaning, and by which we trust God to shape us through all life's experiences for the glory to come.

For further thought and discussion

- To what extent, in your experience, do we live in a pain-avoiding culture? What is good or bad about that?
- Think of a painful experience that you have faced. How have you come to understand it, and what helped you to endure it?
- In what ways does suffering build or threaten your relationship with God?
- How do the perspectives of Romans 5:1–5 and Hebrews 12:4–13 shape your understanding of hardship and suffering?

CHAPTER 6

Grown-up morality

"Jesus said it was all right to steal," announced the man of the road
unexpectedly, as I sat chatting with him over a cup of tea. He didn't
explain his train of thought, but I linked it with the fact that I'd just asked
him where he'd got his jeans from. It's not a question I put to every visitor
to our house, but the previous weekend a pair of quite distinctive green
jeans had disappeared from our washing line at the back of the house, and
it seemed more than coincidence that this man was wearing an identical
pair! At this point, however, I became more interested in his theology
than in the loss of my trousers. On further questioning it transpired
that he was recalling the incident of Jesus and the disciples walking on a
Sabbath day through the cornfields, and helping themselves to the ears
of corn (Mark 2:23–28). He deduced that by defending their actions to
the Pharisees, Jesus was saying that if you really needed something it was
all right to take it. I certainly had to admire his biblical knowledge even
if I felt compelled to point out that Jesus was defending their doing it on
the Sabbath, not making a point about theft. However, I'm sure his need
of the trousers was greater than mine.

The complexities of moral decision-making

The incident threw up some very interesting issues. Yes, he had stolen
the trousers—but did his need as a homeless man in any way qualify that
action? Could there be occasions when it was right to steal, or might it
at least be the lesser of two evils if, say, a poor person stole food to feed
their family? Are laws rigid and absolute, or needing to be interpreted in
each situation? It could be that the man's reasoning was just self-serving

and manipulative, but equally the commandment "Thou shalt not steal" could be a very blunt instrument and not say everything that needed to be said about a situation. When the apostle Paul talks about stealing, he sets it in the context of something more positive: "Anyone who has been stealing must steal no longer, but must work, doing something useful with their own hands, that they may have something to share with those in need." (Ephesians 4:28). Useful work is presented as the antidote to stealing, in order to allow for generosity towards the needy—and therefore, presumably, making it unnecessary for them to steal. There's a lovely circle of grace there which goes a lot further than just the stark commandment. In the absence of generous provision for the needy, is it stealing that is wrong, or the culture that makes it necessary? I'm not presupposing particular answers to these questions, only raising them to point up some of the complexities of moral decision-making.

Furthermore, it raises some issues about Jesus. Among a significant number of religious leaders he was seen as a law-breaker. "We know this man is a sinner," they say to the man born blind, healed by Jesus on the Sabbath (John 9:24). He certainly seemed to sit lightly to contemporary Sabbath observance—in this case, challenging the understanding that plucking ears of corn counted as work. He even alluded to a controversial Old Testament incident when David had eaten the consecrated bread from the sanctuary at Nob, bread that was meant only for priests. He implied, therefore, that human need could override the details of the ritual law. He then concluded the encounter which Mark relates with the principle, "The sabbath was made for humankind, and not humankind for the sabbath; so the Son of Man is lord even of the sabbath" (Mark 2:27–28, NRSV), suggesting that law had to be a servant and not a master, that it needed human understanding and interpretation, and that he, in particular, brought something that went beyond mere legalism.

Going beyond legalism

Rules in themselves do not create a moral or responsibly mature life. The business writer Charles Handy wrote these painfully insightful words about growing up at school:

> Whoever it was who said that your schooldays were the happiest days of your life must have been either a masochist or had a very bad memory, I reflected as I left my last school on my last day. I hoped fervently that it wasn't true, otherwise I was going to have a very sad life.
>
> I left persuaded that the world thus far was unfair, punitive and unpleasant. The best way to survive was to find out what the rules were, to keep your head down and pass the tests that the authorities set you as best you could. It was not the best way to prepare for the independent life, but that was the last thing I was thinking of. I was going to another institution, a university, which would, I trusted, provide me with the credentials for further institutions where I would endeavour to keep the rules and pass their tests until death or retirement overtook me.[54]

Keeping the rules and passing the tests is hardly an inspiring vision or recipe for an attractive or mature life. If it is a sad reflection on some of the trends in education, it can also be where some versions of the Christian life end up. Certainly my early childhood thinking about God was linked with keeping the rules—do this, don't do that—as this moralistic God became an extension of parental control. My thinking did progress to the need to go to church to say sorry for not keeping the rules adequately, but there was a lurking worry along the lines of, "What if, at the end of my life, I died on a Saturday night . . . a whole week of failure unconfessed!" Of course, we can smile at such naïve, childish attitudes but actually a version of this, even if a bit more sophisticated, can carry over into adulthood. The essential point is that a relationship with God is seen as dependent on human performance, and when thinking is that way round, then legalism is never far away. The gospel turns it all on its head, saying that human performance is dependent on a relationship with God.

Jesus and law

It is important to note that Jesus was not against the law. In the Sermon on the Mount his teaching is clear on this:

Do not think that I have come to abolish the Law or the Prophets; I have not come to abolish them but to fulfil them. For truly I tell you, until heaven and earth disappear, not the smallest letter, not the least stroke of a pen, will by any means disappear from the Law until everything is accomplished. Therefore anyone who sets aside one of the least of these commands and teaches others accordingly will be called least in the kingdom of heaven, but whoever practises and teaches these commands will be called great in the kingdom of heaven.

Matthew 5:17–19

All that would have been relatively uncontroversial, with only a slight concern, maybe, over what he meant about himself fulfilling the law. It was the final statement that would have triggered the bombshell: "For I tell you that unless your righteousness surpasses that of the Pharisees and the teachers of the law, you will certainly not enter the kingdom of heaven." (Matthew 5:20). They were the upholders of the law par excellence. They *were* concerned with detail—the smallest letter and the least stroke. They were committed to practise and teach it. Yet Jesus is saying that this was not enough for the kingdom of heaven. So in what ways did Jesus think they fell short?

What follows on from this is a whole series of ethical issues which Jesus introduces with, "You have heard that it was said . . . But I tell you . . .". At first sight it looks as if he might be overturning traditional laws and coming up with a new ethic. On closer inspection it is not that he is contradicting the existing law, but rather taking it further and in so doing making it far more demanding. In some cases, it is about moving it on from outward actions to inner attitudes as well: it's not just "Don't commit murder," but "Don't get angry or abusive with others"; not just "Don't commit adultery," but "Don't look at a woman lustfully." In other cases it's adding positives to negatives: "Don't just avoid angry words but go and get reconciled with your brother"; "Don't just take proportionate revenge, eye for eye and tooth for tooth, but do good things to those who wrong you." In still other cases it's about doing much more: "Don't just love your neighbour, but love your enemy as well."

In all this, Jesus was clearly raising the bar very high, and it would be easy to conclude that this made keeping the law *impossible*. This was, in many ways, the opposite to the concerns of the Pharisees and teachers of the law to make it more *possible* for people to keep the law, initially for very good reasons. So rather than just have big abstract principles, like keeping the Sabbath holy, they spelt out exactly what that might mean in terms of what constituted work. They wanted it to be practical. The trouble was that the detail, rather than being an outworking of the principles, ended up replacing the principles: "You give a tenth of your spices—mint, dill and cumin. But you have neglected the more important matters of the law—justice, mercy and faithfulness." (Matthew 23:23). Law degenerated into a legalism that became an end in itself, focusing on outward, observable, often negative, and ultimately manageable behaviour. Jesus said that it was what came from the inside that was more important: the motivations and intentions behind outward behaviour. He summarized the law as love—loving God with everything, and your neighbour as yourself. "All the Law and the Prophets hang on these two commandments." (Matthew 22:37–40).

It's easy to be unsympathetic towards the Pharisees. We have had years of reading the Gospels, where their opposition to Jesus and unattractive legalism gets the full treatment. However, they set out with good intentions. They wanted the law to be kept, and to help people to do that. If we're honest, most of us would not get close to the standards of Jesus. But then maybe that's the point. Maybe the law is, in some ways, meant to be impossible, to be slightly beyond our reach . . . at least in our own strength. Jesus hints at that in his parable of the tax collector and the Pharisee. The proudly confident Pharisee displays all the characteristics of legalism, concentrating on the negative: "I am not like other men, robbers, evildoers, adulterers . . . "; and on the outward: "I fast twice a week and give a tenth of all I get." (Those on the 5–2 diet, please note.) The tax collector simply comes with the words, "God, have mercy on me, a sinner" (Luke 18:9–14). It is out of this sense of failure, Jesus says, that the man is justified before God.

Law and relationship

Knowing our need of God is the first step to doing the right thing. This was the apostle Paul's great discovery. This Pharisee had been as zealous as any in his law observance but found it an inadequate means of righteousness. In the end, all it could do was reveal his need of Christ: "So the law was put in charge to lead us to Christ that we might be justified by faith. Now that faith has come, we are no longer under the supervision of the law." (Galatians 3:24–25). I think we all know how relationship is a much better motivator than rules. Of course, as parents we set rules for growing children, starting with physical safety boundaries: "Don't touch the fire," "Don't run out into the road," and moving to social boundaries: "Don't take Jack's toys," "Don't tell lies," and so on. When they respond with the inevitable question, "Why?", sometimes we're driven to the only answer, "Because I say so," but always we're trying to build relationship and to give reasons for the rules, until they have to some extent internalized them. The success of that will depend on how much they see care and consistency behind them. So, on a spiritual level, Paul talks of dying to the law so that "the life I now live in the body, I live by faith in the Son of God, who loved me and gave himself for me." (Galatians 2:20). A loving relationship was more effective than law in inspiring the moral life.

I remember once attending a Quiet Day in the private chapel of a large country house. The leader was wanting to make the point that at the heart of biblical theology was story as much as doctrine or law. Spontaneously (at least, so it seemed) he turned to face the east wall and pointed to the list of the Ten Commandments painted on it. "It's all story," he reiterated. For a moment I didn't grasp his point. Surely if anything was not story but rather prescriptive law, it was the Ten Commandments. "Where do you get story out of them?" I thought. However, he only had to read the opening lines to make his point: "I am the Lord your God who brought you out of Egypt, out of the land of slavery." (Exodus 20:2). The Ten Commandments were the continuation of God's great act of deliverance for his enslaved people. It was as if he were saying, "I am the God who brings you freedom. If you want to stay free, then this is how you do so." These foundational laws were set in the context of a liberating relationship.

The importance of boundaries

So does grown-up morality go beyond any rules or laws? No—setting boundaries is a good thing, and rules can define the boundaries. The person without any boundaries will lack a strong sense of their own identity and will struggle with social relationships. In their very practical book *Families and How to Survive Them*, Robin Skynner and John Cleese discuss this theme in terms of parenting children:

> **John** . . . Why *do* they want clear lines?

> **Robin** They feel secure if they know how far they can go. Children like achieving, learning, being stretched a bit, and they also feel safer if they know just how much they can relax and fool around too. So they're much happier if there's enough structure to help them control themselves.

> **John** I'm getting a mental image about how the child feels. I see the child sitting on a chair in the middle of a dark, unfamiliar room. And the child's got to have the courage to leave that chair and explore the room. But it's murky, he's not quite sure where the walls are. But he needs to be able to go off and explore and come up against them and establish where they are, good and firm and clear. Then he can explore the room full of curiosity and without fear. But if the walls *aren't* there he'll get scared . . . Perhaps if he goes too far he'll fall over the edge![55]

The boundaries are important. Far from restricting exploration and growth, they make it possible, they create the space to grow. However, if drawn too tightly they become restrictive and more likely to be ends in themselves than protectors of creative space. Keeping the rules becomes more important than inhabiting and enjoying that which they define, and virtue becomes more about pleasing the lawmakers (parental, religious, or societal) than celebrating the life the rules are designed to enable. We are back with legalism and Handy's vision of a life "keeping the rules and passing the tests". In such a context, growing up may involve breaking the rules, at least in the eyes of some, especially if those rules are more about control than freedom and maturity. Some of the best children's stories involve children overthrowing the unjust or oppressive systems that the grown-up world has imposed on them. Roald Dahl, for instance, is a master of this gentle anarchy.

"Sin boldly"

Potentially just as shocking (and also capable of misunderstanding) were Martin Luther's words when advised by his friend Philip Melanchthon to act cautiously on some of the implications of his new teaching, in case he was getting it wrong. He famously replied, "Sin boldly." Of course, the context is all-important. What he wrote was, "If you are a preacher of grace, then preach a true and not a fictitious grace; if grace is true, you must bear a true and not a fictitious sin. God does not save people who are only fictitious sinners. Be a sinner and sin boldly, but believe and rejoice in Christ even more boldly, for he is victorious over sin, death, and the world. As long as we are here (in this world) we have to sin . . . "[56] I don't think he is saying that sin doesn't really matter, nor that we should not care how we live because God will always forgive us. His target is rather the human respectability and even hypocrisy that is a denial of sin. There is also a sense of, "Live boldly even though you will sin, because the reality of God's grace is larger than any sin we might commit." It was a warning against a cautious over-scrupulousness which, through anxiety about getting it wrong, ends up paralysing action and initiative, and ultimately avoids taking risks. Such anxiety is not going to help us mature, as Jesus demonstrated in the temple at the age of 12.

Luther's words spark all sorts of interesting reflections. First, he raises the possibility that sin can be "fictitious". We have noted how maturity may involve overthrowing some of the understandings of sin imposed on us by others. This may also include fictitious guilt or shame. When children experience life negatively in the early world of dependence, they may find it safer to conclude that it is their fault rather than that of their parents, carers, or significant others in the wider world. To conclude that those on whom they depend so fully are, in fact, undependable is potentially a terrifying prospect, and so false guilt or shame is assumed to keep the world safe. Growing up in *such* circumstances will involve gaining a more realistic awareness of the fallibility of everyone, even those closest to us, and not assuming misplaced responsibility for everything that goes wrong!

Furthermore, Luther's encouragement to be a sinner reminds us that our outward virtue is not always as purely motivated as it seems. There can be a fictitious goodness as well as fictitious sin. We may just be too cowardly, sometimes, to put our darker inclinations into action, or be constrained merely by what others might think. In fact, we may not want to spoil our own self-image as good or upright or faithful and join the common band of those who mess up and get things wrong. The danger of virtue is that the better we are at it, the more likely we end up as proud and insufferable. The invitation to "sin boldly" is a plea for reality rather than deceit, honesty rather than hypocrisy. I remember hearing a prison chaplain, interviewed about his work, being asked what he found to be the difference working with prisoners. "They just got caught," was his sardonic reply.

Sin, humility, and discerning the way of compassion

The miracle of the gospel is the way that God brings good out of evil and uses our failings to engender compassion and love. As Martin Smith puts it:

> As long as pride wants to separate us from others, the Spirit of God has to sabotage our attempts to get rid of sin from our lives. If we continue to fall again and again, at least there is a chance of our breaking through in the end into a humble sense of solidarity with others in their weakness and enter the way of compassion.[57]

Real virtue emerges out of the grace that meets us in our falling, as much as from self-righteous effort. The result is a patient acceptance of ourselves and a carefreeness exhibited in people like the monk Brother Lawrence, of whom it was written:

That when an occasion of practising some virtue offered, he addressed himself to God, saying, Lord, *I cannot do this unless thou enablest me*: and that then he received strength more than sufficient. That when he had failed in his duty, he simply confessed his fault, saying to God, *I shall never do otherwise, if thou leavest me to myself; 'tis Thou must hinder my falling, and mend what is amiss.* That after this, he gave himself no farther uneasiness about it.[58]

If virtue and moral goodness are about inhabiting the space defined by certain boundaries, the question remains as to the extent to which those boundaries are absolute or whether they can be redefined as we grow in our moral responsibility and awareness. How much has God revealed fixed boundaries of acceptable behaviour? How much are they left to human discovery and application? What is the ongoing place of law in Christian living? We have noted how Jesus affirmed the importance of the law, yet was accused by his enemies of being a lawbreaker. His interpretation of what was right could vary considerably from the norms of his day, and he could distinguish between principles and their more detailed application. If that process of interpretation was clearly a mark of Jesus' life, to what extent was it unique to him, or is it a part of every person's or community's journey? When Jesus said that the Sabbath was made for people, not people for the Sabbath, and so "the Son of Man is Lord even of the Sabbath," was his reference to the Son of Man indicating his own unique authority to interpret the law, or was it suggestive of a more general *human* responsibility to do so? And if the Sabbath is made for people, does that suggest that people have a real place in determining how it works out?

The New Testament would seem to encourage believers to live boldly and imaginatively through the grace of God in Christ, letting the Spirit within them interpret the big principles underlying the law. So as Paul seeks to describe the "freedom for which Christ has set us free", he emphasizes "grace" and "faith expressing itself through love", calling people to "serve one another humbly in love. For the entire law is fulfilled in keeping this one command: 'Love your neighbour as yourself.'" (Galatians 5). Grown-up morality can never avoid the responsibility of discerning the meaning of love in any situation. Indeed, sometimes relying solely on the law as if it were absolute can be a failure to exercise that responsibility, a failure to grow up. The implication of Luther's words are that it is better to take risks of love and sometimes get it wrong than to shelter behind a cold, risk-free morality. So, for instance, it would seem entirely right and biblical to affirm that marriage is for life, and divorce is contrary to the will of God. However, to conclude that it is therefore always right for a couple to stay together, or that remarriage can never be contemplated in church, is to fail to do the necessary working through of the principles of grace, compassion, and mercy in any particular situation. In fact, that process was happening in the life of the early church, so that the more absolutist command in Mark ("Anyone who divorces his wife and marries another woman commits adultery against her") is tempered by the additional phrase in Matthew, "except for sexual immorality" (Mark 10:11, Matthew 19:9). In an imperfect world, judgements have to be made as to the right way forward drawing on more than just a legal rule, even if the rule is an important part in the discernment process.

There will be a need, then, for constant discernment—is this action loving and grace-filled or exploitative and self-serving? Just as the Sabbath was there to prevent the exploitation of labour but not to prevent the healing acts of Jesus, so we need to judge any law with a prayerful Christian mind. Furthermore, in an age when the tendency will be to emphasize individual freedom, it is important to stress the corporate nature of that discernment, to guard against the self-deception that can easily justify our behaviours. The New Testament is strong on actions being weighed not just on their rightness for the individual but according to their effect on others, including the "weaker" brother or sister. "Be careful . . . that the exercise of your freedom does not become a stumbling-block to the weak," writes Paul to the Corinthians (1 Corinthians 8:9; see also Romans 14). An action may be wrong because it puts an obstacle in the way of another: drinking in front of an alcoholic, shopping in ways that exploit producers or those in retail. Right behaviour can never be simply what is right or permissible for me. The defiant response to the horrific shootings at the offices of the *Charlie Hebdo* magazine in Paris championed the unconditional right of freedom of speech, and that certainly is a precious gift to be defended in the face of barbaric terrorism. Yet equally, there can be an arrogant and adolescent defence of that freedom which is saying, "I can publish what I like, irrespective of what offence it might cause to others." Beyond independent freedom is a mature interdependence that negotiates liberty according to the needs of others.

A grown-up morality will value risk-taking for the kingdom of God as more important than a defensive purity or legalism which keeps life narrowly under our control. However, it will always be open to corporate wisdom, whether that is found through the guidance of the law or the discernment of the church, for in the end the goal of the kingdom is not just personal happiness or fulfilment, but right and just relationships in transformed communities.

For further thought and discussion

- As you read this chapter, note anything that excites you, or puzzles you, or challenges you. You might want to mark these with a "☺" or a "?" or a "!". Talk about your responses.
- Based on the story of the man's theft of trousers, how would you answer the question, "Could there be occasions when it is right to steal, or at least for it to be the lesser of two evils?"
- How would you define legalism? To what extent is it about getting the right balance between principles and detail?
- Read Luke 18:9–14. Imagine the Pharisee turning to Jesus and saying, "At least I try and do the right thing." What do you think Jesus might have said? How does this fit with Jesus' words in the Sermon on the Mount (Matthew 6:19)?
- "Be a sinner and sin boldly, but believe and rejoice in Christ even more boldly." (Martin Luther). How do you understand and apply his words?
- Can you give an example of where you have changed or might change your behaviour out of consideration for "the weaker brother/sister"?

CHAPTER 7

Grown-up guidance

Some years ago, I spent quite a long period of time seeking out the will of God for my next sphere of ministry. It felt time to move, but the doors just didn't seem to be opening. It led to the inevitable soul-searching as to what I was really looking for, how I was coming across at interview, and then—at times—the deeper questions about where God was in it all and whether he had a purpose or "right place" for me, which I just had to be patient in discovering. When some of this was at its height, and I was feeling quite frustrated and discouraged about the whole process, I found myself at a conference; on the last day these feelings came particularly to the fore in my awareness. I remember saying to God in prayer, "I just feel stuck."

The conference was to end with a communion service, and one of the organizers asked me if I would be willing to anoint people with oil after they had taken communion, as a sign of God commissioning them for service back in their parishes. Slightly hesitantly I agreed, and then they added, "And say any words you feel God gives you for them." "Well," I thought, "God hasn't exactly been making his will known to me recently;" but the service duly began, and while a couple of us got involved in the anointing, I did find myself being given a thought or a word for people as they came. When we had finished, the other person anointing turned and asked me to anoint him. I did, and then thought I had better say, "Please anoint me." I didn't have much faith that anything would happen, but I thought it would look a bit proud not to ask. So he did—and then he added these words: "May God lubricate your way so you are no longer stuck." I was amazed; without knowing anything about my situation, his words had pinpointed my need exactly, even using the word of my earlier prayer. It felt a massive sign that God was in the situation and that I could trust him for the future.

Not long afterwards, I found myself with two further interviews just two days apart. They were interesting jobs, and I ended up being offered them both! The familiar analogy of London buses came to mind. In fact, I found myself feeling quite irritated. After waiting all this time, suddenly I had to decide which of these two jobs was right. I wrestled in prayer, spoke to those who knew me, and eventually the only thing I could sense God saying was, "You choose." In whatever way he was guiding me—and my conference experience had encouraged me to believe that he was— there was still room for choice, still a need for knowing my own heart and making an adult decision. Discovering the will of God felt not so much like listening to a set of instructions, but rather creating a future together.

Discovering the will of God

The idea of discovering the will of God can be understood in very different ways. We can approach it from the starting point of *what* God wants us to be doing—and that can range from the very big life decisions (What is my vocation? Who should I marry? Should I have a family?) to the more mundane (What are the priorities for today?). These will, of course, relate to each other. If we believe God has called us to translate the scriptures into an obscure language, then our days will be organized into tasks enabling us to do that. If we believe God is calling us to be a foster-parent, then family will rightly dominate our lives. Temperament and personality will play a part here. Some will be big-picture people, like the person who asked me at a job interview, "Where do you see yourself in ten years' time?" This was presumably to test out my ambition, but it potentially betrayed a rather worldly approach to vocation. Some will have a much more immediate focus, looking for God's direction in the everyday, responsive to the Spirit's more direct prompting. However, it can also be argued that God's will is as much about *how* we live our lives as *what* we are actually doing: the moral purpose and shape to any particular actions. Certainly that is the perspective caught in Micah's famous words: "And what does the Lord require of you? To act justly and to love mercy and to walk humbly with your God." (Micah 6:8). In practice, content and character need to go together in any seeking after the will of God.

Many, though, will start with the idea that God has a general plan for their lives which they need to discern and obey. The scriptures are full of stories of those whom God has called for a particular purpose, whether it be a prophet like Jeremiah who heard God say to him, "Before I formed you in the womb I knew you, before you were born I set you apart; I appointed you as a prophet to the nations" (Jeremiah 1:5), or Esther who is challenged by her uncle to speak up for the Jews, "For . . . who knows but that you have come to your royal position for such a time as this?" (Esther 4:14). Old Testament prophets looked forward to the day when God's immediate purpose and leading would be known: "Whether you turn to the right or to the left, your ears will hear a voice behind you, saying, 'This is the way; walk in it.'" (Isaiah 30:21; see also Jeremiah 31:34). The apostle Paul encourages the Ephesians to see themselves as "God's handiwork, created in Christ Jesus to do good works, which God prepared in advance for us to do" (Ephesians 2:10).

Sometimes the stakes can be raised when the word "perfect" is linked with God's will, as in a verse like Romans 12:2 which invites us "to test and approve what God's will is—his good, pleasing and perfect will". While this is chiefly about testing the goodness of God's moral purpose by not conforming to worldly pressures, it's a short step to imagining that God has a perfect plan for our lives, and that our task is to do our best to get ourselves into it. If that initially sounds exciting and adventurous, it can quickly become quite a burden. The main trouble is that it's a very static image—you are either in the plan or not—and it doesn't offer much help for when things go wrong. What happens when we make a mistake, or take a wrong turning, or are on the receiving end of the mistakes and inadequacies of others? It is not an image that fits easily with the complexities of real life.

A redemptive partnership

Such thinking can make us essentially backward-looking, striving to regain some lost perfection, rather than forward-looking, working with God to realize a new future. In a life which will always contain a measure of incompletion and imperfection, a more helpful way of seeing God's purpose is not as some perfect blueprint or standard to which we are always striving to return, but as a day-by-day redemptive partnership where good things are created in a relationship of grace. In fact, it is noteworthy that the Bible is essentially a salvation history rather than a story of paradise regained, the continuing redemption of a flawed and vulnerable people rather than a catalogue of success.

Jesus Christ announces the coming of a kingdom which is both "already" and "not yet", both here and still to come. Even the Garden of Eden only merits half a chapter in Genesis and has an evolving dynamic rather than a static perfection. Humanity is created from the dust of the ground with the responsibility to cultivate and take care of the garden, working on the earth to enable it to reach its full potential, and taking care of it to restrain the forces that would destroy it and make it revert to chaos and nothingness. The naming of the animals seems to symbolize the mandate given to humanity by God to direct creation towards its goal and purpose, and away from the chaos to which it might return.

John V. Taylor has pointed out how formative for the Old Testament people of Israel was the experience of redemption:

> ... what launched the Hebrew tribes into their distinctive faith was an experience of the impact of rescue: the religion of the Old Testament sprang out of the Exodus from Egypt. God had kept a promise. God had saved. God was to be trusted. The stories of their earlier ancestral origins in the days of the patriarchs and the dim, mythical period before that, as we have them in the Bible, were all told from the settled life of the Israelites in their own land, and the telling bears the mark of the never-absent memory of that Exodus. Even their accounts of the creation of the world and the making of humankind are set down in terms that recall that definitive experience of rescue.[59]

This redemptive emphasis even shapes the descriptions of creation. So Isaiah can describe creation as almost the first act of redemption. The prophet exhorts God to act:

> Awake, awake, arm of the Lord, clothe yourself with strength! . . .
> Was it not you who cut Rahab to pieces, who pierced that monster through? Was it not you who dried up the sea, the waters of the great deep, who made a road in the depths of the sea so that the redeemed might cross over?
>
> *Isaiah 51:9–10*

Creation, expressed as the slaying of the dragon of chaos, is depicted in the same breath as the exodus from Egypt. God redeems a world from chaos, even as he redeems Israel from their slavery.

Again, Jeremiah is given a picture of God as he watches what the potter does when the pot he is making is marred in his hands. Rather than discarding or destroying it, he forms it into another pot, shaping it as seems best to him. "Like clay in the hand of the potter, so are you in my hand, O house of Israel." (Jeremiah 18:1–9). God is constantly starting again from where his people are: redeeming, reshaping, renewing. Furthermore, the new possibilities are very dependent on his people's response—if he is acting in judgement and the people repent, then he will relent from the disaster he planned; if he is acting to build up the people and they do evil, he will reconsider the good he intended to do.

Living with incompleteness

We once had the privilege of a family holiday around California, and as part of it we drove out to see the Grand Canyon. For me it was the highlight of the trip—one of the most awe-inspiring natural phenomena I have witnessed. However, we were only there for twenty-four hours, and when we arrived, in the late afternoon, there was only time for a few preliminary views and a dash out with rather a lot of others to a good viewpoint for some sunset photos. On the next day, as we planned to walk down into the canyon, we encountered dire warnings about going too far, both because of the heat and because you did the downhill first and then had to come up again. As we had children to think of, then a thunderstorm threatening, we only walked—for an hour or so—a little way into the canyon. By the time we left, in spite of loving what I'd seen, I was feeling really depressed because I'd not had the *complete* experience of the Grand Canyon, as I saw it, and I imagined that I might never come there again.

It was then that I realized I was falling into a way of thinking that was quite characteristic—whereby I was measuring everything by a standard of perfection, and then feeling sad or guilty if experience didn't measure up, which often it didn't. What was a "complete experience" of the Grand Canyon anyway? Would there not be many experiences to be had, depending on the season or the weather or the mode of transport—helicopter or mule or on foot—and most importantly, the company sharing the experience? I was setting myself up to fail or to be disappointed. As we have seen, the Bible rarely sets a perfect scenario for us to attain. It presents life as a redemptive adventure whereby, in partnership with God, we discover, shape, and perfect the future. From God's omniscient perspective that may constitute a plan, but from a human point of view it is much more helpful to see it as a journey of redemptive discovery.

"It seemed good to the Holy Spirit and to us . . . "

There is a lovely phrase in the New Testament, used to describe a decision of the early church, that seems to give expression to this partnership: "It seemed good to the Holy Spirit and to us . . . " (Acts 15:28). The context is the discussion at the Council of Jerusalem about whether Gentiles coming into the church had to be circumcised and keep the Jewish law. It can sound, at first, like one of those rather esoteric religious debates, but in fact it had huge implications for how the early church related to the world around it and understood its mission. Although this was a turbulent moment for the church, and an issue about which passions ran high (as we discern in some of the epistles), there is a measured wisdom and authority conveyed in these words, "It seemed good to the

Holy Spirit and to us . . . ", the fruit of an attentiveness to God combined with a mature human judgement. What were the components of this discernment of God's will?

First of all, the church leaders spent time noticing what God had been doing (see Acts 15:4, 12–14). Paul and Barnabas were able to report the evidence, out in the field, of what God had done through them among the Gentiles, revealing himself in remarkable ways with many responding in faith. That provoked Simon Peter to recall the extraordinary occasion when he was led, through visions and dreams, to the house of the Roman centurion, Cornelius, entering it in a way that was unthinkable for a Jew, and finding a group of Gentiles so open and hungry for the gospel that he was only midway through his sermon when the Holy Spirit dramatically fell upon them all. On this occasion, God didn't wait for the prayer of commitment (or, for that matter, the Alpha Day Away, or the confirmation service). Through the Spirit, he came to them and initiated their repentance and faith. At the council they took time recalling and remembering these things.

Then secondly, they reflected on the scriptures in the light of these things, and on these things in the light of the scriptures (vv. 15–18). Seeing how the early church interpreted the new things God was doing in the life, death, and resurrection of Jesus, and the birth of the church in the power of the Holy Spirit, through the lens of their Old Testament scriptures is a fascinating and complex study, but it's instructive to see how consistently they sought to do that. We have seen how, throughout the New Testament, they seemed to expect their experience of God to be informed, shaped, and interpreted by the scriptures.

Thirdly, having noticed what God was doing, and reflected on it in the light of the scriptures, they made a reasoned and grace-filled decision, as expressed by James: "It is my judgement, therefore, that we should not make it difficult for the Gentiles who are turning to God." (v.19). So they refrained from demanding adherence to the Mosaic law and all its rituals, only asking for certain points to be observed. Peter's argument had been persuasive, suggesting that they were testing God by "putting on the necks of the Gentiles a yoke that neither we nor our ancestors have been able to bear" (v.10). The image of the yoke recalls the words of Jesus: "Take my yoke upon you and learn from me, for I am gentle and humble in heart, and you will find rest for your souls. For my yoke is easy and my burden is light." (Matthew 11:29–30). There is a gentleness in the call of Jesus that will not load us with demands that we cannot bear. There will be a fit with who we are, a resonance with our deepest desires and profoundest longings.

How easy is God's will?

Is this, then, an important mark of God's will, that it does not feel difficult or even impossible? I want to say a qualified "yes". But then does this mean that if something is not only going to be good to the Holy Spirit but also *to us*, it is going to be agreeable, attractive, even easy? How much is some degree of feeling good about it important for being in God's will?

I think it is right that God's will should seem good to us, should excite us, fulfil us, give us joy; but of course, the phrase "seeming good" can signify quite a complex reality. I have already confessed that there is a part of me that thinks something can't be right unless it's difficult or painful, and can't be of God unless it hurts a bit. Such thinking is rightly suspect. Yet we are called to "take up our cross" and follow Jesus, and to "enter through the narrow gate", and certainly for me, ministry has at times taken me right to the edge of my resources, to a sense of being overwhelmed by the expectations or responsibilities, the exposure of a public ministry, or the discouragement of opposition or indifference. We may be stretched to the limit in following the will of God. The paradoxes that abound in the New Testament give expression to this complexity. You find them in Paul, especially in 2 Corinthians: "dying, and yet we live on" (6:9), "sorrowful, yet always rejoicing . . . having nothing, and yet possessing everything" (6:10), "when I am weak, then I am strong." (12:10). You find them in the Gospels: "Anyone who loves their life will lose it, while anyone who hates their life in this world will keep it for eternal life" (John 12:25). And especially in the Beatitudes: "Blessed are the poor in spirit . . . Blessed are those who mourn . . . Blessed are you when people insult you, persecute you and falsely say all kinds of evil against you . . . Rejoice and be glad . . . " (Matthew 5:3–12). These paradoxes suggest that Christian life and calling is potentially going to feel infinitely demanding and satisfying at the same time, good to us and yet threatening everything we are. Clearly, knowing what is good is going to take some discerning.

God's will is always going to connect with the reality of who we are; we don't have to try to be anyone else, and that's really good news. The trouble is we don't always know ourselves that well, or find it easy to be ourselves. We can discover that we're acting out some sort of role we think we ought to assume, or that others expect us to, out of pride or fear or a desire to control things. Over the years, we may have imbibed a message that what we are is not enough, it is inadequate. Sometimes our sense of self will be very much shaped by the roles we are performing— spouse, parent, child, employee, minister, or whatever. Sometimes the roles become so familiar that we can lose touch with who we really are, and so don't always know what feels good to us. We have to please, or we have to be the peacemaker, or we have to be the rebel, or the awkward one, or the one to sort things out. Being ourselves is both simple and yet very demanding.

On another occasion when I was considering moving jobs, I was rung up by a retired army officer, inviting me to come and see him about a parish of which he was the patron. I was living in Wolverhampton at the time, and found myself having the rather surreal experience of driving down to Bath to learn about a parish near Derby that I had never heard of. From his description, I didn't expect much to come from it and so, after a nice lunch, I attempted to extract myself with a polite and suitably pious-sounding conclusion along the lines of, "Well, I'm sure God will guide me and you in the decisions that we have to make." He clearly wasn't impressed. "Well, if you don't mind me saying so," he retorted, "he's made a few bloomers before now!" I was suitably shocked at the implication that God makes mistakes, but of course, he may well have been reacting to my spiritual pomposity, and he was right that seeking or even claiming the will of God is no guarantee of success. Guidance is a divine-human partnership and we only know ourselves imperfectly. While I'm sure God sometimes rescues us from our worst decisions, mistakes clearly happen, and they become part of the redemptive journey of our lives. We will always be learning and growing in who we are, and what seems good to us can change.

The Council of Jerusalem reached a point of decision about God's will for the Gentiles by attending to what God was doing, listening to the scriptures, and resolving not to make it unnecessarily difficult for them to join the church. If we are going to seek God's will for our lives in a similar way, then attending to factors such as circumstances, what others are saying, the scriptures, and our desires and hopes will all feature in the mix. However, I don't think it's helpful to get too fixated on "the perfect plan".

There is an archetypal story from ancient China which suggests we should not be too quick to imagine a situation is contrary to God's purpose or outside his will. A poor farmer has a horse to plough his fields, but one day the horse gallops away. A neighbour commiserates with him, saying, "That's bad news." The farmer replies, "Good news, bad news, who knows?" A few days later the horse returns, bringing several wild horses with it. "Good news", you might say. But the farmer's response was the same: "Good news, bad news, who knows?" The farmer's son tries to tame one of the wild horses, but while riding it is thrown off, breaking his leg. Neighbours console the farmer: "Sorry for your bad news." Yet still the farmer replies, "Good news, bad news, who knows?" A week later, the emperor's army enters the village and takes every able-bodied young man to fight in a war. The farmer's son is spared. The farmer's response? "Good news, bad news, who knows?"

The story makes clearly the point that understanding and evaluating circumstances is not easy, and faith in the redemptive power of God in any situation is a more trusting response. This is certainly the thrust of the oft-quoted words from Romans 8:28: " . . . we know that in all things God works for the good of those who love him, who have been called according to his purpose." They acknowledge vocation and purpose, but encourage trust in God working through all circumstances. Alongside trusting God is knowing ourselves, so that our understanding of what "it seemed good to us" consists of is deeper and more real.

Some have likened God's purpose to a tapestry where one side presents a beautiful, coherent picture, but the other side reveals a jumble of threads and colours, apparently without order. Maybe there is a perfect plan, viewed from God's eternal perspective. However, from our perspective we need to trust that the mixture of the good and bad that the world throws our way, alongside the wise choices and mistakes we make, can be woven by God into a calling and purpose that he can use to his glory and our fulfilment.

For further thought and discussion

- When have you been conscious of being guided by God, and how did he make his will known?
- What are the strengths and weaknesses in the idea that God has a plan for your life? Are there other models of understanding God's guidance and direction?
- When Jesus said, "My yoke is easy", to what extent was he saying that God's will for our lives will always feel good and manageable? How much does God fulfil our desires?
- Can we trust God to be working out his purpose for us in all circumstances (Romans 8:28)?

CHAPTER 8

Grown-up Jesus

Although I was brought up in a churchgoing family, and my faith was certainly real at different points of my childhood, it only really took off when I went to university. I was fairly ignorant of different types of church at the time. On the first Sunday, I went with others to a large evangelical Anglican church which was familiar enough, even if the evangelistic call at the end of the sermon was a new experience for me. On the second Sunday, however, someone I had met said they were going to try out a local Pentecostal church, and I innocently decided to join them. I don't remember a lot about it except that it was like nothing I had ever encountered before, and at the time I was very unsettled by it. However, one detail does remain in my mind. Towards the end, I recall the leader giving a "word" (which I now realize was a word of prophecy), which was along the lines of someone needing to step out from the safe world of their parents into a new relationship with God. I don't think I gave it much attention at the time. There was enough to process in the whole experience of Pentecostal worship. But the fact that I remember it suggests that it had registered somewhere inside me, and looking back, I think it was a fairly accurate summary of what was happening at that particular point of my spiritual and emotional journey.

I also remember that as I took those early steps of spiritual independence, it was never easy talking about it with my father. Somehow, we always seemed to end up arguing. After one such argument I remember reading a verse from Psalm 51 which says, "You desire truth in the inward being; therefore teach me wisdom in my secret heart," (v.6, NRSV), and feeling convicted that my new-found understanding had not yet been adequately incarnated in my life and behaviour. With hindsight, I think I was probably being a bit hard on myself. But in there was a dilemma: in the Ten Commandments was a clear instruction to respect and honour parents, and yet it felt that going forward in my spiritual life and vocation required a measure of rebellion and changed allegiances. Negotiating that transition was not easy.

Jesus and family

We noted in the first chapter how little material there is in the Gospels about Jesus' childhood. We cannot, therefore, observe his growing up, or his emerging character and developing spirituality. Apart from the brief incident in the temple when he was twelve, we don't know whether it was always smooth and straightforward or sometimes bumpy and tempestuous. Were there family rows and arguments, or perpetual respect and sweet agreement? Was Jesus essentially a conformist or a rebel?

The likelihood, of course, is a mixture, and that would seem to be confirmed by what we see of Jesus as an adult. Certainly his relationship with his family is portrayed as robust. If there were signs of that in the early temple incident, it continues at the wedding in Cana, when Jesus reacts to his mother's concern about the wine with the comment, "Woman, why do you involve me?" (John 2:4). He did, of course, go on to get spectacularly involved.

However, the time when the relationship really does have some edge is when his mother and brothers arrive at the house where he is in a sharp discussion with the teachers of the law (Mark 3:20–35). We have already heard that the busyness of his ministry is getting in the way of proper mealtimes, and his family are clearly worrying that he is going over the top, losing perspective, and even getting fanatical. "They went to take charge of him, for they said, 'He is out of his mind.'" So when he is told, "Your mother and brothers are outside looking for you," he is almost cruelly dismissive. "Who are my mother and my brothers?" he asks. We don't know if his question got back to them as they stood outside. There were plenty of people to report it. However, as it hung there, there must have been quite a sense of shock in the air.

In the end, Jesus answers his own question. As he looks at the crowd sitting around him, he says, "Here are my mother and my brothers!

Whoever does God's will is my brother and sister and mother." It is a new family that engages his attention and commitment now, the community of those who are pursuing the agenda of a heavenly Father. At this moment, the priority of the new family requires a radical distancing from his original family of birth. He has to become his own person before God, in the company of others committed to the same. He will teach that discipleship calls people to a first loyalty to him: "Anyone who loves their father or mother more than me is not worthy of me." (Matthew 10:37).

Jesus' question in Mark's Gospel—"Who are my mother and brothers?"—is a very searching one for all disciples. Where do my ultimate securities and loyalties lie? To what extent do my beliefs and actions reflect my upbringing, or the values of the kingdom? It is like the words spoken by the Samaritans to the woman who introduced them to Jesus: "We no longer believe just because of what you said; now we have heard for ourselves, and we know that this man really is the Saviour of the world." (John 4:42). Growing up into the children of God involves going beyond what we hear from others, including our own parents and family, and understanding and experiencing Jesus Christ for ourselves.

This is not to say that Jesus abandoned his biological family. As he hangs on the cross, his mother is part of a group of women watching nearby, and in a moving and tender moment the dying Jesus entrusts her to the care of "the disciple whom he loved", thought to be John (John 19:26–27). Furthermore, it would be extraordinary if such respect and care were missing, as the principle of honouring your mother and father was written deeply into Jewish culture, enshrined as it was in the Ten Commandments, where it appears with the promise, "that you may live long in the land the Lord your God is giving you" (Exodus 20:12). Again, it is particularly striking that the last words of the Old Testament look forward to the day of the Lord, when Elijah will "turn the hearts of the parents to their children, and the hearts of the children to their parents" (seen by Luke to be fulfilled in John the Baptist: Malachi 4:5–6, Luke 1:17). This is contrasted with "striking the land with total destruction". I could imagine many themes other than family harmony and reconciliation forming the final words of the Jewish scriptures and being singled out as signs of the Messianic age. Moreover, I am surprised by how the alternative is portrayed as so catastrophic. This, then, was the milieu in which Jesus lived.

So I do not see Jesus diminishing the importance of family, but instead putting it in its right position as a servant of the new community that he was forming around himself. Thus, when his family come to "take charge of him", he has to take a stand and resist the pressure to mould him according to their needs and priorities. Family can take charge of us in all sorts of ways. It may be through actual relationships and tangible pressures. However, there will also be internalized scripts and expectations, attitudes and rules of behaviour which we will have imbibed in our upbringing, and which will be shaping the people we are and the way we live. Failure to conform may elicit accusations of ingratitude, disloyalty, and even betrayal, engendering feelings of guilt, even shame within us. Any journey to maturity has to revisit those things and test them against the freedoms and priorities of being children of God. Unless we uncover those inner rules and bring them into the light of our relationship with Christ, they will compromise our growth into the unique people God has called us to be.

Of course, we will undoubtedly have inherited good things from our families too, and they will be bearing fruit as well. The test is the degree to which we feel constrained or controlled by family rather than free to be ourselves. It is certainly very striking to see how much Jesus was his own person. He stood up to the pressures of his family. Even though he enjoyed friendships and was particularly close to the inner group of his disciples (Peter, James, and John), when Peter tried to dissuade him from the path of suffering and rejection he called him "Satan". It is particularly remarkable to note how he was able to handle the pressures of popularity and stay true to himself and to what he felt called to do. Early in his ministry, he had a particularly successful evening when, in Capernaum, "The whole town gathered at the door, and [he] healed many who had various diseases." (Mark 1:32–39). The next day he set off early to pray, but people clearly wanted more, and Simon and his companions went to look for him. "Everyone is looking for you!" they told him, with the implicit, "Come on, we're on a roll here! We need to stay with this." Which of us in ministry wouldn't interpret such blessing as a call for more? Not so Jesus. He answers, "Let us go somewhere else—to the nearby villages—so

I can preach there also. That is why I have come." Success was not going to alter his sense of priority. Again, after recording that "many people saw the signs he was performing and believed in his name," John notes, "But Jesus would not entrust himself to them, for he knew all people." (John 2:23–24). Here was a man with an astonishing capacity to act with an inner authority and not to be pushed around, either by admirers or his enemies. Was he simply unique, or were there ingredients in his own maturity from which everyone can learn?

Attitudes to authority

There is a story from the Second World War of the time when an important ship was sunk off Crete. Several craft, it seems, were involved in taking the survivors to Alexandria, and after many hours at sea, the sub-lieutenant in charge of the landing craft was ordered once too often to make another trip out to sea. He got on the phone to head office and proceeded to sound off about the order. "What the ***** are you playing at? Don't you know what state the men are in? It's all very well for you sitting back at HQ," and so on. The voice at the other end replied with a solemn authority, "Do you know who you're speaking to? The Commander-in-Chief of the Western Mediterranean." There was a short pause before the sub-lieutenant seemed to resume his belligerence. "And do you know who you're speaking to?" he asked. "No," came the reply. "Thank God," he said, and slammed the phone down.

Obedience is a high priority in the military, and the angry protests of the junior officer are rapidly withdrawn when he realizes that it is his commanding officer on the other end of the phone. There cannot be much space for questioning in the life-and-death scenarios of war, where a strong sense of hierarchical authority is an essential component of securing action in difficult or dangerous circumstances. Yet we warm to this sub-lieutenant's spirit and suspect that his forthright plain speaking was part of his effectiveness as a soldier rather than some sign of disloyalty.

Such a model might be thought to be inappropriate to the mature life of faith, and yet there are resonances here with the Gospel story of another military man, the centurion who came to Jesus to seek the healing of his servant. Displaying the thought processes of his position, he invites Jesus just to give an order rather than actually coming to the house: "For I myself am a man under authority, with soldiers under me. I tell this one, 'Go,' and he goes; and that one, 'Come,' and he comes. I say to my servant, 'Do this,' and he does it." Far from putting Jesus off by his manner, he is commended for his faith: "I tell you, I have not found such great faith even in Israel." (Luke 7:1–10). The centurion's faith in Jesus is linked to his experience of effective authority in the military. There it comes from knowing his place in the chain of command—being under authority himself so that his orders to others carry the authority of the whole institution. Far from stifling effective action, this seems to release it.

The centurion recognizes and demonstrates the link between being under authority and the freedom to act with authority. Getting the issue of authority clear engenders a sense that anything is possible, anything can be done, and Jesus clearly warms to that faith. So often, attitudes to authority can seem to get stuck on one side or the other—either a rather passively obedient conformism or a rebellious and self-serving individualism—whereas the centurion seems to offer a model that fuses the best of both. Finding creative approaches to authority is a vital task for today's church, which is dividing over its emphases and understandings of different authorities, be they scripture, human reason and experience, or the tradition of the church.

One of the remarkable characteristics of Jesus was the authority with which he spoke and acted. People noticed it right from the start of his ministry:

> The people were amazed at his teaching, because he taught them as one who had authority, not as the teachers of the law . . . The people were all so amazed that they asked each other, "What is this? A new teaching—and with authority! He even gives orders to impure spirits and they obey him."
>
> *Mark 1:22, 27*

What was it about Jesus that led to this favourable contrast with the current religious teachers? The conventional wisdom is that their teaching was all a bit derivative and second-hand, quoting learned rabbis but lacking a sense of personal engagement and integrity . . . all sermons off the Internet rather than applied wisdom from the school of life and the school of prayer! Theirs was not leadership from the inside out, whereas when Jesus taught, people had a sense of freshness, authenticity, and embodied wisdom and holiness. Even his enemies say, "Teacher, we know that you are a man of integrity. You aren't swayed by others, because you pay no attention to who they are; but you teach the way of God in accordance with the truth." (Mark 12:14). They may have been laying a trap through their flattery, but the picture had to be recognizable to succeed.

However, even Jesus, who acted with such personal and direct authority, seemed to have an awareness of being "a man under authority" as well. This is very evident in the account of one of his most controversial acts of rebellion and protest against the religious establishment of the time, when he marches into the temple courts and drives out those buying and selling there, overturning the tables of the money-changers and the benches of those selling doves for sacrifice. It would appear to be a spontaneous act of prophetic indignation, a dramatic, visceral outpouring of righteous anger, where the legitimacy of the authorities is challenged by this one man's alternative vision for the temple. However, while all that is clearly there, there are also other interesting parts to the narrative, especially as Mark tells it (Mark 11:11–33).

Mark, alone of the synoptic Gospels, does not place the clearing of the temple immediately after Jesus' triumphal entry into Jerusalem. Instead, Jesus looks around at everything in the temple area, but because it is late departs to Bethany for the night. The implication is that he has seen things that will bring him back, and overnight he has time to reflect on how he might act. So he does return to Jerusalem the next day, stopping on the way to curse the fig tree that hasn't delivered the fruit to assuage his hunger, even though it was not the season for figs. It would seem to prefigure his actions in the temple, which had also become unfruitful, and would ultimately wither under the judgement of God. Soon no one would eat fruit from there again, either. Yet from a human perspective,

Jesus' words reveal the emotional tension inside him that morning, as he went to confront the situation he had observed in the temple the night before. This was an out-of-season fig tree, not the temple, yet Jesus was angry that it could not satisfy his hunger.

Passionate as he was, Jesus had still reflected on his intended actions and the authority which he had to engage in them. Even as he cleared the temple, he explained his actions by saying, "Is it not written . . . ?" It is a familiar phrase in his teaching, revealing a deep awareness of the scriptures and a deep respect for their authority. Here, at the climax of a highly charged situation, it is the scriptures that are used to justify his actions, just as they had been essential at other crucial moments of his life, such as his resistance to the temptations in the desert.

Then, in the aftermath of the temple incident, the religious leaders come and confront him specifically on the question of authority: "By what authority are you doing these things?" (v.28). His reply is mischievously incisive. He will only answer if they can tell him their view on the baptism of John. Was it from heaven, or of human origin? It proves to be an inspired question, for they are caught either way. John bore witness to Jesus, therefore to acknowledge his divine authority would be to concede that of Jesus also. However, because John was such a popularly acclaimed prophet, to dismiss his authority would put them at odds with the prevailing mood. So they cannot answer. The interchange reveals how important it was for Jesus to be anchored in a tradition, and not a "lone ranger" or self-appointed prophet. He surprised people—including John himself—when he submitted to John's baptism, and yet the symbolic importance of it and the accompanying testimony of John are shown to be highly significant in these later confrontations. Jesus could act with seemingly unique and original personal authority. Yet this was set in the context of deep respect for the scriptures and of the endorsing testimony of others.

The authority of scripture

If that powerful combination of acting with freedom and authority, yet from a place of respect and submission to others' authority, was a hallmark of Jesus' life and ministry, he also expected the same of others. So we find him responding with some exasperation to the rather tortuous arguments of the Sadducees about the resurrection with a curt, "Are you not in error because you do not know the Scriptures or the power of God?" (Mark 12:24). It would seem that Jesus expected their understanding of truth to be found through the scriptures, and also through what they were experiencing of God in their lives. In fact, I suggest he was linking the two. How we read the scriptures will be shaped by what we are experiencing of God, just as what we experience of God will be shaped by the scriptures. In the case of the Sadducees, their closed and conservative rationalism disabled them from seeing God's possibilities.

In this way, the scriptures are a bit like a map. When I go walking, I usually look at the map and plan a route, but often I will then encounter things on the journey that make me go back to the map and see something I hadn't noticed before, or see it in a new way. Or sometimes I will just set out walking, and then go to the map afterwards to help me understand where I've been. The scriptures are constantly guiding, shaping, and interpreting our experience according to the reality and purposes of God, even as our experience also shapes what we find in the scriptures. There may be some who are uneasy about the idea of our experience shaping what we find in or understand from the scriptures. Yet not only is this integral to how the scriptures came into being in the first place, but it also points to the continuing dynamic of human translation, interpretation, and application.

My own evangelical tradition has strongly championed the primacy of scripture, but has not always recognized its bias. When I was writing on the charismatic renewal that has been such a significant movement in the church, and researching the issue of spiritual experience, I came across some words of John Stott which shocked me. He said this:

The revelation of the purpose of God in Scripture should be sought primarily in its *didactic* rather than its *descriptive* parts.

> More precisely, we should look for it in the teaching of Jesus, and
> in the sermons and writings of the apostles rather than in the
> purely narrative portions of the Acts.[60]

This was highly significant, for the narrative portions of the Acts do actually yield a theology of spiritual experience. Again and again in Acts, we see the early church gaining profound theological insights from their experience, as they encounter God leading them in new and often surprising ways. In fact, this was the genesis of most doctrine as the apostles reflected on their experience, albeit in the light of the scriptures. Ruling out narrative as a source of the revelation of the purpose of God is to carve a massive hole in the biblical canon and to ignore the fact that interpreted story is a key source of how the Bible presents truth. John Stott was rightly a giant in the evangelical world, and I admired him enormously, yet here there seemed to be a selective use of scripture that was serving his particular argument.

Growing up in our faith is to recognize that there are no infallible sources of authority which bypass our humanity, whether the scriptures or the tradition of the church. I believe that the scriptures are inspired by God, able to make us "wise for salvation through faith in Christ Jesus" (2 Timothy 3:15–17). We can never study them too much! Yet Jesus has to warn the Jews, "You study the Scriptures diligently because you think that in them you have eternal life. These are the very Scriptures that testify about me, yet you refuse to come to me to have life." (John 5:39–40). He was, of course, referring to the Old Testament, but the principle is the same. Even diligent study of the scriptures could fail to bring recognition of the person that they were all about, because in the end it involved their humanity, with all its cultural conditioning, self-justifying tendencies, and partial perceptions. For us, too, it still needs real spiritual renewal to accompany it, constant humility to recognize alternative perspectives, and the company of others to balance or challenge current orthodoxies. While we might have expected Jesus to make orthodoxy the test of authenticity, he actually opts for something far more experiential: "By their fruit you will recognize them," he teaches in the Sermon on the Mount (Matthew 7:20), asserting in the last discourses in John's Gospel that "All will know you are my disciples if you love one another." (John 13:35).

The dynamic of scripture and experience is vital. Ignore scripture, and we are in the quicksands of relativism where anything goes; ignore experience, and the narrow dogmatism of "infallible" interpretation leads to a diminished life where our own bias goes unnoticed. Jesus was always quoting scripture, it seems, from the beginning to the end of his ministry. It was vital to his countering of the temptations in the desert, and was on his lips as he died. Yet he also pointed beyond to a relational and behavioural discipleship that the scriptures were there to engender. He was a man under authority, acting with authority, yet increasingly at odds with authority. He upheld the importance of the law, yet responded to the issues of his day with creative freshness and insight, constantly pushing the boundaries of Sabbath, or of generous human relationships and inclusivity.[61]

The grown-up Jesus was difficult to put in a box. Sometimes he was conformist, sometimes rebel, depending partly, no doubt, on the perceiver. He burst the boundaries of his upbringing, both relationally and behaviourally, yet took scripture seriously and pointed to those who pursued obedience to God as his new family. He was his own person, yet embraced friendship and fellowship. So how does the church of Jesus Christ become a grown-up church?

For further thought and discussion

- What good things do you feel you have inherited from your family, and what feels more difficult?
- Read Mark 3:20–35. In what ways does your family "take charge of you", that is, dictate how you think or feel or act? With whom do you commit to do God's will (v.35)?
- Was Jesus a conformist or rebel, individualist or team player, man of the book or free thinker? What about you?
- What can we learn from Jesus about the place of scripture in mature discipleship?
- "By their fruit you will recognize them." What sort of things might you look for to indicate authentic and true maturity?

CHAPTER 9

Grown-up church

The importance of community and church

Maturity is created in community and tested by community. Yet community attracts and scares us at the same time. We can long to belong to others, and fear the isolation of being alone. Yet we can also fear belonging to others, that it might mean the loss of identity or the pressure to conform to another's expectations or control. However, if we want to grow up into our full personhood we cannot avoid the risk of community. There is no solitary maturity.

It is very striking how quickly the priority of community appears in the Bible narrative. The word "good" features many times in the opening verses of Genesis, with the refrain of the first chapter: "God saw that it was good," "God saw that it was very good." So it comes as a shock when into this idyllic description there suddenly enters a contrary assessment: "It is not good . . . " (Genesis 2:18). What was not good? It was not good for the man to be alone.

So there was something "not good" in the human condition before sin entered the world, and that was isolation, or aloneness. There was something "not good" even when the man stood in an unspoilt world and in an unbroken relationship with his creator. The beauty and resourcefulness of creation was not enough; the creativity and responsibility of work was not enough; a perfect relationship with God was not enough. There was still something "not good", and it was all to do with being without human community. In Genesis the antidote is the creation of woman, leading to the institution of marriage. "For this reason a man will leave his father and mother and be united to his wife, and they will become one flesh." (2:24). However, in the New Testament the apostle Paul broadens the application of this to the community of the church. "This is a profound mystery," he says, "but I am talking about Christ and the church." (Ephesians 5:32).

It is perhaps unsurprising that Paul reaches such a conclusion, given that his first encounter with Jesus Christ had been as he made his way angrily to arrest the believers he found in Damascus. As he does so, he is arrested himself by a blinding light and a penetrating question: "Saul, Saul, why do you persecute me?" When he asks for the identity of the voice, he hears simply, "I am Jesus, whom you are persecuting." (Acts 9:3–5). Hearing the voice of Jesus must have been disturbing enough. The realization that such was the Lord's identification with his followers that his persecution of the church was no less than a persecution of Jesus himself must have been a shocking revelation. Perhaps it was the foundation of his great metaphor for the church as the body of Christ. We need the church to be fully Christian. We need community to be fully human. When the church gets it right, there is something hugely attractive and compelling about the community it creates.

Creating community, however, is a big challenge, and not surprisingly, in a consumer culture which gives the message that life must fit around me, many avoid that challenge. The mantra today of being "spiritual but not religious" is played out in many individualistic faith journeys that bypass the church. However, this is no reason for smug superiority on the part of those who persevere with organized religion. Often the church community has been closed and unwelcoming to the stranger looking in, or even to the dissident in the fold. If church is part of the deal for mature faith, then we need to discern the factors that will make it life-giving. What will a church of grown-up children look like?

Status and service

The organization of any community brings us up against issues of power, authority, and status. Who makes the rules? Who controls the entrance? Who gives significance? As we observe Jesus and his disciples in the Gospels, it is evident that handling issues of power and status is vital. The disciples argue about who is the greatest, or the most important, or the most powerful, and Jesus has to point them to the priority of service. Unlike secular leadership of the day, they are not to lord it over each other but to serve one another. There will be something childlike in their relationships, with a mutual service that will undercut powerful hierarchies.

I tried to dramatize this once when preaching at the ordination of deacons in our cathedral. Our bishop was shortly to retire, so I invited him out, along with the young son of one of the ordinands, and spent a few moments extolling the achievements and qualities of our episcopal leader. After a slightly exaggerated but largely true picture of the bishop, I turned to the boy and said, "Jonny, Jesus says to you that if you want to become a successful Christian leader, you must aspire to become like him." It sounded reasonable, but I could tell in the silence which followed that it was dawning on some that this wasn't quite right. After a suitable pause, I made the explicit connection with the Gospel reading we had heard shortly before. "No, he didn't say that. He said, 'Bishop, you must become like Jonny.'" " . . . the greatest among you should be like the youngest, and the one who rules like the one who serves." (Luke 22:26).

The community of the church has the particular characteristic of service. As such, we are to be like the Son of Man, who "did not come to be served, but to serve, and to give his life as a ransom for many"(Mark 10:45).

Furthermore, that service is primarily for "the many", the world which Jesus came to save. It is participation in the mission of God. However, the means of that service is a church which models serving relationships in its own community.

It is not always easy to put into words this vision of mission through community. Sometimes, in order to emphasize the distinctive community, we have made the church sound more like a club with rules and membership than the body of Christ in the world. It is to counter such thinking that many quote the words attributed to former Archbishop of Canterbury William Temple: "The church is the only institution that exists primarily for the benefit of those who are not its members." However, that risks downplaying the importance of the relationships within the church community. The church exists for mission, even as it embodies the message of the new humanity that it proclaims.

Lesslie Newbigin began to capture the balance when he said that "the only hermeneutic of the gospel is a congregation of men and women who believe it and live by it". He continues:

> The deepest root of the contemporary malaise of Western culture is an individualism which denies the fundamental reality of our human nature as given by God—namely that we grow into true humanity only in relationships of faithfulness and responsibility toward one another. The local congregation is called to be, and by the grace of God often is, such a community of mutual responsibility. When it is such, it stands in the wider community of the neighbourhood and the nation not primarily as the promoter of . . . social change (although it will be that) but primarily as itself the foretaste of a different social order.[62]

That is some vision for the church.

Jesus' final prayer

It is a vision I see Jesus articulating in the prayer that concludes the "final discourses" of John's Gospel (John 17). It is a prayer about the widening dynamic of the life of God, the eternal life that Jesus has come to give those given to him. It begins in the life of the Trinity, in the eternal love between Father and Son: "Father, I want those you have given me . . . to see my glory, the glory you have given me because you loved me before the creation of the world." It continues through the disciples, the embryonic church: "I have revealed you to those whom you gave me out of the world . . . I pray for them. I am not praying for the world, but for those you have given me, for they are yours." It then issues out beyond them into the wider world: "As you sent me into the world, I have sent them into the world . . . My prayer is not for them alone. I pray also for those who will believe in me through their message, that all of them may be one, Father, just as you are in me and I am in you . . . Then the world will know that you sent me and have loved them even as you have loved me." The ripples extend outwards as the very life of God in eternity is given human expression in the church, and from there into the world.

The interdependent church

The church is the body of Christ, his continuing presence on earth, here to serve the mission of God. But what will this look like? Does our metaphor of grown-up children inform the sort of community we might expect the church to be? For children, it needs to be a place of discovery, nurture, guidance, and care, within a safe context of belonging. For grown-ups it needs to be a place of responsibility, service, and attention to the world beyond itself. Put these together, and we might be looking for a church that is welcoming but not stifling, safe but also stretching, clear but not controlling, united but not uniform, with an ethos of mutual service rather than a division between those who give and those who receive, and porous boundaries between inside and outside.

This is the sort of interdependent church that I see Paul envisioning in Corinth. Within this church, Paul found factions identified around particular leaders—"I follow Paul", "I follow Apollos", "I follow Cephas"— and his first shot is simply to point them back to Christ. "Is Christ divided?" he asks. He develops the theme by recognizing different roles in the God-given growth of the church. "What, after all, is Apollos? And what is Paul? Only servants, through whom you came to believe—as the Lord has assigned to each his task. I planted the seed, Apollos watered it, but God has been making it grow." (1 Corinthians 1:12–13, 3:5–6). However, disunity appears to have run deep within this church and the divisions are manifesting themselves in those who are saying, "I don't really belong here," while others are conveying the attitude, "I don't need you." All the insecurities of community are surfacing, as issues of power and status are played out. However, to our huge benefit it elicits from Paul his great metaphor for the church as the body of Christ, with its powerful vision of interdependence between those with different gifts, and the so-called strong and the weak. He challenges those who are saying, from a sense of superiority, "You're not an eye—I don't need you," and those who are saying, from a sense of inferiority, "I'm not a hand—I don't belong."

The pride and fear behind the negative attitudes of "You are not, I am not
. . . " are to be subsumed by the reality that "you are the body of Christ,
and each one of you is a part of it." (1 Corinthians 12:15–27). In God's
church I need you, I belong.

Arrogance can infect any church, whether it be the Church of England,
proud of its establishment, or the latest Fresh Expression, proud of its
independence. It is a danger among evangelicals, perhaps because of the
current strength in numbers. An article in *IDEA* (the magazine of the
Evangelical Alliance), under the title "Do I really need to go to church?",
identified those who have "'ditched' the Church as an obsolete relic from
a bygone age—outdated, irrelevant, decrepit, boring". Wanting to reaffirm
the church's central importance to the mission of God, it continued:

> All of which can be remedied by radical surgery, explosive truth,
> Holy Spirit-empowered believers, bold actions, and faithful
> uncompromising leaders who'll do what Jesus tells them to
> do. We don't need any more wimps, sceptics, hypocrites, child
> molesters, or 'wimpy' clerics too scared to challenge compromise
> that destroy churches, in Jesus's name.[63]

I have no issue with the first sentence. Of course the church needs
courageous leadership. But I become uneasy once it says, "We don't
need . . . " Soon we are saying, "We don't need you . . . unless you're on
the top of your game," "We don't need you, unless you are Holy Spirit-
empowered," "We don't need you unless you believe like us . . . "

By their fruits

A grown-up church can live with the reality that Christ is enough to
make me a Christian, not Christ plus my zeal, or my orthodoxy, or my
church style or order, or my gifts of the Spirit. We belong in Christ and
then are free to allow the particular manifestations of God's grace to grow
in us, for the good of all. At the retreat that preceded my ordination,
I remember the speaker having us all on the edge of our seats when
he announced, "You know, there are really only two sorts of Christian."

He paused for dramatic effect, and in the gap we were all trying to imagine what he was about to say. Would it be Catholic and Protestant, or liberal and evangelical, high church and low church, or traditional and contemporary? However, he just repeated the statement, "There are really only two sorts of Christian," and just as we could take the suspense no longer, he added, "live ones and dead ones".

I have found that to be both amusing and insightful. It really does undercut the fantasy that *my* version of the church is the all-important factor in bringing life and growth. The reality is that there is life and death within all traditions. I think Jesus takes a similar line in the Sermon on the Mount, when he teaches that the true will be recognizable from the false "by their fruit" (Matthew 7:15ff). Some will call him "Lord", but not enter the kingdom of heaven for failing to do the will of the Father. Others will do spectacular, charismatic-looking signs such as prophecy, exorcism, and miracles, but will be dismissed by Jesus as those he never knew. Outward words and actions have to be measured against this test of fruitfulness, which would seem to embrace both character and effects. It is a warning to us that what we add to our definition of a Christian is only authentic if it bears the fruit of Christ-like character and service. Otherwise it can be no more than wanting the security of the tribe, the comfort of the gang.

Mission-shaped unity and diversity

I am encouraged that within the church as a whole there has emerged what I term a "mission-shaped ecumenism", less concerned about resolving all the differences of doctrine or church organization, and more about serving the world and preaching the gospel. If you ask people in a church about their Christian journey, many have moved between different traditions and even denominations at some time. Old stereotypes are being challenged as Protestants find that Catholics believe in personal salvation, while Catholics find that Protestants believe in the church. Evangelicals find that liberals pray, and liberals find that evangelicals are concerned for the world. So even if institutional unity has not moved forward in the ways once hoped, there is often a relational unity today, put to the cause of mission, where diversity is accepted and even celebrated as it becomes an important ingredient of the church's witness. Indeed, just as investment advisors recommend a mixed portfolio of assets to spread financial risks, so I imagine God seeing a diverse church as the best hope of safeguarding a holistic mission to a needy world.

Of course, this does not mean that issues of truth and order are unimportant. An undiscerning tolerance of every way as equally valid may be a welcome departure from the over-authoritarian certainties of the past, but it can lead to a lazy or sentimental discipleship that lacks the robustness to create real community among damaged and divided people, or a credible witness in a complex and confused world. There will be personal and corporate beliefs and disciplines which enable growth, fruitfulness, and healthy fellowship. A celebration of diversity does not mean that "anything goes". In Jesus' prayer in John 17, truth is seen as an essential defence in an evil world. Jesus says, "My prayer is not that you take them out of the world but that you protect them from the evil one. They are not of the world, even as I am not of it. Sanctify them by the truth; your word is truth." (John 17:15–17).

However, truth is not just an abstract propositional concept: it is relational. Jesus said, "I am the truth." He is the "living word". Equally striking in the prayer of Jesus is the emphasis on unity: "that they may be one", repeated three or four times. It can certainly be argued that truth is an essential component of that unity. We unite around shared belief. However, it is also true that unity is an essential component of truth. It is as we commit to shared and diverse relationships that we understand and experience the truth more fully. In another of the apostle Paul's descriptions of the church as the body of Christ, he presents a compelling vision of a community with all engaged in service, equipped by a diversity of gifts and so finding a unity in faith, and knowledge and maturity.

> So Christ himself gave the apostles, the prophets, the evangelists, the pastors and teachers, to equip his people for works of service, so that the body of Christ may be built up until we all reach unity in the faith and in the knowledge of the Son of God and become mature, attaining to the whole measure of the fullness of Christ.
>
> *Ephesians 4:11–13*

Unified diversity is the friend of truth and antidote to idolatry. Here we begin to attain "to the whole measure of the fullness of Christ". Indeed, it is often mixing with those who are different that tests our genuineness and keeps us honest. Loving those who are like us is comparatively easy, and excelling in those situations where we know (or maybe have even created) the rules is much more achievable. It is the people who are different from us, even the enemies Jesus commanded us to love, who really test the depth of our virtue and reveal our need of the grace of God if we are truly going to love as Jesus commanded. The self-righteous church is never far away when we start defining ourselves over against another.

What keeps the church alive?

So if the real issue is about being alive or dead, what keeps the church alive? If we stay with the metaphor of grown-up children, it is about tradition and change, inheritance and growth. The Church of England's Preface to the Declaration of Assent for clergy captures something of this when it says of the church, "It professes the faith uniquely revealed in the Holy Scriptures and set forth in the catholic creeds, which faith the Church is called upon to proclaim afresh in each generation."[64] There is a real interdependence between past and present, the old and the new. One of my great concerns for the contemporary church is its demarcation by age, and therefore the potential idolatry of both tradition and change.

Certainly the church must not be defined by yesterday. This is the warning from the biblical story of the "bronze snake" which became an important instrument of healing in the hands of Moses. The snake was a God-given antidote to the venomous snakes sent among the people as they complained and grumbled against God and Moses in the desert. Jesus himself saw it prefiguring the cross and resurrection: "Just as Moses lifted up the snake in the desert, so the Son of Man must be lifted up, that everyone who believes in him may have eternal life." (Numbers 21:4–9, John 3:14). Yet when Hezekiah begins his "reform and renewal" as king, one of his first actions is to break into pieces the bronze snake Moses had made, for the Israelites had been burning incense to it (2 Kings 18:1–4).

It shows how easily today's blessings become tomorrow's idolatries, or as someone once said, the last seven words of a dying church are, "We have always done it this way."

As I travelled around churches as an archdeacon, I often saw outward signs of yesterday's church: the out-of-date noticeboard (or even the out-of-date website!), the clutter that no one is willing to throw away, the pictures that reflect a bygone era. To be fair, many Anglican churches have to cope with a historic building that is not designed for the contemporary church, and battle with heritage constraints to renew their buildings for mission. The Victorian mindset (and money), with its love for rigid interiors, serried ranks of pews, and hierarchical ordering, is a long way from the values, needs, and expectations of today's culture; the hold this has on many church interiors can be a real stumbling block to life. If buildings reflect our inner values and priorities, we have some work to do.

Equally important is not defining ourselves by negatives—by what we are not. Many groups in history have been stronger on their negative identity than anything else. *The Boy in the Striped Pyjamas* is a moving story (and film) about a secret friendship that develops between Bruno, the young son of the commandant of Auschwitz, and a Jewish boy in the camp. It is never explained to Bruno where they are living or what the camp is, so one day he tries to pump his older sister Gretel for information. She tells him that the people in the camp are Jews, but he is still puzzled, even asking her whether they themselves are Jews. She is appalled and despite giving him an emphatic "no", struggles under his persistent questioning to say who they actually are. In the end, the best she can come up with is to assert that they are "the opposite".[65]

Her answer reveals this tendency to define ourselves over against the other. Too often I've heard a congregation affirmed or defined, in a sermon, through being compared favourably over against others—the traditionalists, the "happy-clappy" brigade, the younger generation, the older generation, the rest of the church apart from us, the bishops or the diocese and so on, all giving the implicit message: "We're the opposite, we're not like that." Usually it is a gross caricature of a group that is being described. It's a cheap win, and is the road to death.

The church has to be defined by Jesus, no more, no less, and as the body of Christ must be living out the interdependence of grown-up children who say, "I need you, I belong." No one is so independent or self-sufficient as not to need others; no one is so dependent or ungifted that they do not have their part. There will be limitless ways of working this out in the life of the church, so let me just give three examples from the core areas of worship, fellowship, and mission.

Interdependent worship

What might interdependent worship look like? I suggest that it will be worship where there is the right balance of giving and receiving. One of the classic scriptural descriptions of worship comes in Romans 12:1, where Paul writes: "Therefore, I urge you, brothers and sisters, in view of God's mercy, to offer your bodies as a living sacrifice, holy and pleasing to God—this is your true and proper worship." It is a reminder that worship is always responsive to the initiative of God, taking place here "in view of God's mercy". It is as we see God that our worship is real and truthful, and as we see him as merciful that it is possible. All worship starts with God, and we need the Spirit to open our eyes and hearts to his truth and love. Worship also, however, requires our wholehearted response: offering ourselves as a living sacrifice. Such a response is clearly active and participative—worship is not a spectator sport—and also costly, demanding the best that can be given.

In my experience it is not always easy to hold together both these characteristics: excellence and involvement. Some churches have the resources to provide worship of a high quality—perhaps through iconic architecture, inspired preaching, beautiful music, or state-of-the-art AV facilities. Others may not have the skills or setting to deliver such an experience, but people are engaged and transformed through their participation. Their leading of prayers, or giving of a testimony, or leading an all-age activity make the worship live, for them as well as others. There is no right or wrong about either model, and as we have seen, both are important parts of worship. We should try to deliver quality, as well as participation.

It helps, though, for a church to have thought through what it is trying to do. My experience is that some churches aim to operate an excellence model when they would be much better offering a participative model. Perhaps they don't have much in the way of resources, such as a great choir or inspirational preachers, but "dwelling in the word" in small groups could be a really helpful exercise,[66] or having a team that tries week by week to portray the theme in a visual way. Those in a well-resourced church will need continually to make sure they are relying on God to inspire them, not just their human talents, and consider how they can counter a passive spectator experience. The participative church may need to encourage training and feedback as people's contributions emerge, and to think how contributions with more enthusiasm than talent are handled. I recall one church asking people who wanted to express their worship in dance and movement to do it at the back, where people were not compelled to watch! However, a truly interdependent church will want to handle these tensions for the benefit of all, and for the sake of worship fostering life and transformation.

Interdependent fellowship

Another expression of interdependence will be seen in the way churches handle the boundaries of fellowship. When I was a curate, I used sometimes to visit parishioners (not just churchgoers) in the local hospital, and once came across a woman who lived quite near me. As I introduced myself, I got an abrupt response: "I don't agree with the Church of England." I wasn't immediately put off, as we might all be able to endorse that statement in part. But on further examination, it emerged that it was particularly "its ministry" that provoked her disapproval. The conversation revealed her to be a person of faith from a rather closed denomination, and we disagreed on a number of issues. However, as I prepared to make an exit I made my customary offer to pray with her, which was rejected out of hand. "That's fine," I said, adding as I held out my hand to say goodbye, "It's been nice meeting you." "I can't shake your hand," she concluded; "that would be having fellowship."

That may be a rather extreme story, but there will be both implicit and explicit boundaries around any fellowship, some more inclusive, others more exclusive. If we are seeking to be defined by Jesus, then to what extent was he inclusive or exclusive in his relationships? The answer to that is not straightforward, as shown by two of his statements which are at first sight contradictory. On one occasion, his disciples are concerned that an exorcist who is "not one of us" is driving out demons, but Jesus tells them not to stop him because "whoever is not against us is for us" (Mark 9:38–41). On another occasion, the Pharisees were alleging that Jesus was driving out demons by the power of Beelzebub, the prince of demons, and Jesus says, "Whoever is not with me is against me, and whoever does not gather with me scatters." (Matthew 12:24–30). Two similar statements, yet conveying a completely opposite tone, the one inclusive, the other exclusive. How do we approach such seemingly irreconcilable statements?

In the first instance, they warn us from ascribing to Jesus too easily either an inclusive or exclusive position. Simple statements like, "Jesus accepted everybody" or, "Jesus only accepted the explicitly faithful" are both inadequate summaries of the Gospel portrayals. Furthermore, the contexts of these sayings suggest a basis for their differences. When Jesus says, "Whoever is not with me is against me, and whoever does not gather with me scatters," he is directing his words at some determined opponents who were linking him with the devil. Such attitudes revealed a wilfulness, blindness, and resistance to God's action in and through Jesus, a blasphemy against the Spirit. To call good evil, and to reject God's chosen deliverer is to shut the door on the means of salvation. There is a chosen path, according to Jesus, in which there is no forgiveness, now or in the future. They are some of Jesus' most sombre and challenging words.

However, "Whoever is not against us is for us" revealed a generous inclusion of those who might have had differing levels of faith, understanding, and commitment, even though not completely identified as "one of us". Jesus can motivate and inspire people's lives at many levels, explicitly and implicitly, and it would appear that he was not possessive about his name if people's actions were well-intentioned and orientated towards others' wellbeing. Furthermore, that action might be very simple and practical. A cup of water given to a disciple in his name would be rewarded (Mark 9:41).

It is never easy for the church to hold together the exclusive and inclusive portrayals of Jesus in the Gospels. So sometimes there has been an exclusive severity in the way the church has reacted to the goodness of the non-believer, or the non-committed. The Church of England's Thirty-nine Articles exemplify this with the harsh evaluation of Article 13: "Works done before the grace of Christ, and the Inspiration of His Spirit, are not pleasant to God . . . we doubt not but they have the nature of sin." It is undoubtedly presented as an important antidote to a sentimental righteousness or a cheap grace. Yet it can easily encourage an exclusive attitude towards where the grace of Christ or the inspiration of the Spirit is at work, and Jesus seems to offer the possibility of a more generous discernment of a person's actions, even before they are fully committed to the visible company of God's people. The church that bears the name of Jesus Christ will look both exclusive and inclusive at different times. It will want to proclaim the uniqueness of Christ, but to be generous in defining the company of his followers; to be clear on the way of salvation, but open to the varied ways in which people get on the road.

Interdependent mission

In fact, an openness to the outsider will be another way of keeping faith alive and real and sharp. Interdependence includes our approach to mission where, in addition to our proclamation of the gospel, we can expect to learn from those with whom we seek to share the gospel. It is arguable that this is what happened to Jesus in his encounter with the Canaanite woman whose daughter was demon-possessed (Matthew 15:21–28). It certainly happened to Peter in his encounter with Cornelius. Paul Bayes writes:

> For [Professor Walter] Hollenweger the story of Peter and Cornelius as told in Acts 10 was a formative text. He would say "Here we read of the conversion of Cornelius; but surely we also read of the conversion of Peter." Peter's vision of the sheet full of unclean creatures, and of the voice of God declaring God's creation clean, radically changes him. Changed as he is, he opens himself to an encounter with Cornelius and his friends that changes him further . . . [67]

It is also characteristic of one of the great mission stories, appropriately named *Christianity Rediscovered*, where Vincent Donovan tells of how his understanding was changed by the Masai tribes of East Africa. Having challenged them to move, like Abraham, beyond the patently tribal god they follow, he is asked, "This story of Abraham—does it speak only to the Masai? Or does it speak also to you? Has your tribe found the High God? Have you known him?" Before he can give a glib answer he recollects the many ways Western countries have allied Christianity to their national cause—in France, in Germany, in America—and then finds himself saying:

> No *we have not* found the High God. My tribe has not known him. For us, too, he is the unknown God. But we are searching for him. I have come a long, long distance to invite you to search for him with us. Let us search for him together. Maybe, together, we will find him.[68]

"Maybe, together, we will find him" could be the mission statement of an interdependent church for grown-up children. It will no doubt sound too tentative for some. However, it asserts the biblical truth that we will not find him alone. We need others, both within and beyond the church, to keep our faith alive and growing. We need to have scope to give and receive, to say "I need you" and "I belong". We will welcome diversity, for that has the potential to show us more of Christ and to help the church define itself by him, rather than by the non-essentials of culture or tribe.

For further thought and discussion

- "We need the church to be fully Christian. We need community to be fully human." How would you defend that view in an individualistic age when many define themselves as "spiritual but not religious"?
- "The greatest among you should be like the youngest, and the one who rules like the one who serves." (Luke 22:26). How is that worked out in practice?
- How, in your experience, does the church balance being a fellowship that relates well and deeply with the call to give itself away in mission to the world?
- Why do people feel, "I don't belong", and how can we make people feel, "I don't need you"?
- How would you define a "live" church as opposed to a "dead" church?
- Is the search for truth helped or hindered by being in a diverse church?
- What are the strengths of the excellence model and the participative model in worship, and which is better for your church?
- Are you an inclusive or an exclusive church, and is that helpful and right?
- "Maybe, together, we will find him." In what ways is that a good attitude to have in relation to mission?

CHAPTER 10

A faith that keeps on growing

A television newsreader was giving a lecture in the cathedral on God in Africa, and in the question and answer session that followed was asked about his own beliefs. He had been brought up in a Catholic home, but clearly in adulthood he no longer had an active faith in God. However, there was no obvious antagonism towards his childhood faith, and he even went on to say, "I envy people of faith. I wish I had that sort of certainty."

On the surface I could understand what he was saying. I had heard people declare similar aspirations before. It presents itself as a sincere conclusion for someone who, while feeling perfectly warm towards people of faith, cannot quite find enough evidence in their own experience of the world to take up that position for themselves. It can sometimes emerge from people who have experienced the darkness of life, which they cannot integrate with belief in a good or active God. More often it comes from those who experience life as basically good, and don't feel any need to go beyond human causes to explain it. I wonder whether, in reality, people are distancing themselves as much from the religious framework with which faith is packaged as from the thing itself.

In this case, there was an interesting mixture of the two. Here was a man who, as a journalist in Africa, had seen some of the worst aspects of human life—genocide, famine, corruption, war—enough to make anyone hard or cynical. Yet he seemed to have emerged with a strong faith in human goodness and potential. I wanted to understand that more, so I asked him a question about evil, but that was not a concept with which he resonated. Maybe he just had a very positive temperament. Maybe he was in some way living off the capital of his religious background. Maybe as a journalist he was more storyteller than philosopher or theologian.

For whatever reason, he did not perceive himself as a believer yet envied the certainty of people of faith.

However, for me his conclusion was unsatisfactory on several fronts. In the first place was his view of faith as certainty. I know there are some scriptures which seem to equate the two, such as the beginning of the chapter in Hebrews celebrating the heroes of faith: "Now faith is being sure of what we hope for and certain of what we do not see."(Hebrews 11:1). There are other translations that modify this: "the assurance of things hoped for, the conviction of things not seen" (NRSV), "confidence in what we hope for and assurance about what we do not see" (NIVUK). I like the phrase in *The Message*: "It's our handle on what we can't see." It is our means of connecting to something that goes beyond normal evidence. However, even in the translation using the word "certain", it is clearly being used in a particular way. The arresting oxymorons stand out: "sure hope", "unseen certainties". These are concepts that are not usually put together—like "bitter-sweet" or "exact estimate". If we are talking about certainty, it will not be in the usual obvious way, because in some ways faith is the opposite of certainty. It is exercising trust in something (or someone) that goes beyond our visible experience of the world. It is our "handle on the unseen". If it is too certain, it ceases to be faith.

However, I have a greater difficulty with the expression, "I envy people of faith." It is like someone saying, "I envy your fitness." It suggests there is nothing that can be done about it. You're either fit or you're not. You either have faith or not. You're lucky if you do. If faith, though, is a "handle on what we can't see", we need to start turning it, just as if we're going to get fit, we need to start exercising. Faith is not a static concept. It can grow or diminish, depending on our experience and our willingness to test it out.

The importance of faith in the Gospels

As we read the Gospels we find quite a nuanced and subtle portrayal of faith. It is clearly a very significant factor in what Jesus was able to do. When the woman who had been subject to bleeding touches Jesus' cloak and is healed, he says to her, "Daughter, your faith has healed you." (Mark 5:34). However much we know that it was really about Jesus, he himself points to her faith. Then when he goes to his home town, we read, "He could not do any miracles there, except lay his hands on a few people who were ill and heal them. He was amazed at their lack of faith." (Mark 6:5–6). His power to act was hindered by the unbelief of the over-familiar locals. Again, a father brings to Jesus his son who is possessed with an evil spirit, or rather he brings him first to the disciples, who cannot do anything, drawing out the rather exasperated retort from Jesus, "You unbelieving generation . . . How long shall I put up with you?" To the man's plea, "If you can do anything, take pity on us and help us," Jesus replies, "If you can? Everything is possible for one who believes." (Mark 9:17–23). All these responses indicate that faith was hugely important in what Jesus was able to achieve through his ministry.

However, there are also dangers in such thinking. It can be only a short step to a mindset that makes our experience of God more about us than about him, more about the quality or size of our faith than the power or character of the God we are seeking to trust. Imagine a situation where a walker gets into difficulty high on the fells, and as the mist comes down and he gets more and more lost, he eventually manages to phone Mountain Rescue, who come out and get him to safety. That night as he shares his experience in the pub, he is heard to say, "It was my mobile phone that saved me." We know what he means, but at best it is only shorthand. A member of the rescue team overhearing him might rightly protest, "No, son, it was us who saved you." If there had been no Mountain Rescue, he would still be out on the fells. The phone was important, but only as the point of connection.

I say "only as the point of connection" when of course, both the phone and the team were necessary to achieve the rescue. It's just that the team is clearly primary and the phone is the means of connecting to it. It is interesting to note Jesus' response when the apostles come to him and say, "Increase our faith!" He replies, "If you have faith as small as a mustard seed, you can say to this mulberry tree, 'Be uprooted and planted in the sea,' and it will obey you." (Luke 17:5–6). Far from focusing on an increased faith, he talks about what might be achieved with a small faith. Maybe he is wanting to point to what is primary and what is just the connection. Faith in itself is not as important as where that faith is directed and in whom it is placed. Otherwise we may as well be saying that it doesn't matter what or who we believe in, as long as we believe. We have faith in faith itself.

One of the most interesting responses comes from the father challenged by Jesus with the words, "Everything is possible for one who believes." His very real and, in fact, faithful reply is, "I do believe; help me overcome my unbelief!" (Mark 9:23–24). It is enough to release Jesus' power to deliver. It also shows us something of the essence of faith. There is continuing vulnerability and the man in no way comes over as cocksure or presumptuous. He admits the struggle, and hence the turning to God. This is faith in God emerging from human helplessness, even from a struggle to believe. It is not some working-up of human confidence or positive thinking, and it is not certainty. It is experimental faith, turning to God even when unsure how much good it will do.

Justification by faith

There is inevitably something circular in the growth of faith. We cannot know exactly where we enter that circle, and where God's initiative and our response begin and end. Faith is both a gift of God and that which lays hold of the gift. Our faith can grow as we exercise it, but the more it does, the more we will be conscious of God rather than ourselves. The great insight of the Protestant Reformation was justification by faith. It is a liberating truth that our right standing before God comes through faith in Jesus Christ and not by observing the law.[69] It is the ground of huge hope and assurance that our weakness and vulnerability do not have to frustrate the purposes of God in our lives. Yet even the phrase "justification by faith" can be heard to imply that it is our faith that is all-important, and that can be presented to mean our grasp of the doctrine, our correct understanding of the truths, or our ability to believe in these things. Subtly our faith can become the focus, rather than just the connection to a merciful, empowering God.

Paul puts it most helpfully when he writes, "Therefore, since we have been justified through faith, we have peace with God through our Lord Jesus Christ, through whom we have gained access by faith into this grace in which we now stand." (Romans 5:1–2). The key phrase is "access by faith into this grace". The grace of God is our foundation, where we find our footing. Faith is the way in, the handle to the door.

Faith and doctrine

How, then, does faith relate to doctrine? Of course, how we understand God will be an important component in our faith. Our ability to trust someone will depend on what we think about them. We need to grapple with truth if faith is going to be real and liberating. However, there can be an over-intellectualizing of truth, making faith no more than an assent to a body of facts. As a young Christian I was given the illustration of three people walking along a narrow wall—facts, faith, and feelings. Faith was in the middle, with facts out in front and feelings behind. As long as faith kept looking ahead at facts, we were told, it would stay steady on the wall. If it started looking behind at feelings it would quickly fall off. This was fine in making the limited point that faith was more than just feelings, and that sometimes we had to trust God even when we didn't feel his presence. What it didn't say was that faith needed more than just facts, as well, and that our feelings might give an equally important access into the truth of a situation. I have learnt that it is much more insightful, and in the long run exciting, to make sure we are noticing our feelings and asking where they are coming from, what they are saying, and where God is in relation to them. Sometimes that will need to happen in the company of a friend or counsellor, who by their empathy and attentiveness can help us express and understand what is going on.

Over-intellectualizing faith will exaggerate the importance of knowledge rather than trust. It will tend to see faith as a set of truths to learn, and the danger is that once that becomes the most important criterion, then to gain assurance we need to define truth quite rigidly. A saving faith becomes linked to certain right doctrines, which are defended fiercely because assurance depends on them. Growth in faith becomes about grasping the basics more fully, rather than taking that understanding more deeply into our own interior lives or more widely into the culture of the world around us. Such churches can be very good on initial evangelism, as they teach the basics well. However, that is where they get stuck, and eventually people get bored with the lack of application and development. A growing faith will risk new insights, new applications, new emphases. In fact, justification by faith enables risk and experimentation because we know that getting it wrong is not the end of the world. Justifying faith is revealed, according to Jesus, in a tax collector beating his breast and saying, "God, have mercy on me, a sinner." (Luke 18:13–14).

Good, sound teaching is a great gift. Many Christians could do with more. Yet faith requires more than that. As Rick Warren puts it: "The *last* thing many believers need today is to go to another Bible study. They already know far more than they are putting into practice. What they need are *serving* experiences in which they can exercise their spiritual muscles."[70] For this reason, I would define faith as action based on trust. Truth and understanding are a component of that trust, but trust is ultimately a relational concept which will be revealed in actions. Growth in faith will involve growth in our ability to apply faith to our lives, to grow in self-knowledge and our ability to trust, to grow in love and service.

Faith and works

This takes us into the central New Testament tension between faith and works. Read Paul, and it would seem to be all about faith. Read James, and it would seem to be all about works. Both look at the life of Abraham and draw their conclusions from it. Paul's focus is on how Abraham continues to believe in the promise of a child, even when he and his wife Sarah are way beyond child-bearing years.

> Yet he did not waver through unbelief regarding the promise of God, but was strengthened in his faith and gave glory to God, being fully persuaded that God had power to do what he had promised. This is why "it was credited to him as righteousness." The words "it was credited to him" were written not for him alone, but also for us, to whom God will credit righteousness—for us who believe in him who raised Jesus our Lord from the dead. He

was delivered over to death for our sins and was raised to life for our justification.

Romans 4:20–25

Abraham continued to trust God, even when the fulfilment of the promise had become humanly impossible, and it was credited to him as righteousness. It is the same for us when we trust in God's mercy and grace offered through the death and resurrection of Jesus, in the face of the moral impossibilities of the law. Works of the law cannot justify us before God, says Paul, only grace received through faith.

However, the extent of our trust will always be revealed in what we actually do. Works are the outward indication of faith. This is what the letter of James states so clearly:

> Show me your faith without deeds, and I will show you my faith by what I do . . . Was not our father Abraham considered righteous for what he did when he offered his son Isaac on the altar? You see that his faith and his actions were working together, and his faith was made complete by what he did. And the scripture was fulfilled that says, "Abraham believed God, and it was credited to him as righteousness," and he was called God's friend. You see that a person is considered righteous by what they do and not by faith alone.
>
> *James 2:18–24*

It is interesting that James chooses a more active example from Abraham's life: his willingness to sacrifice his son Isaac. This reveals the faith that is credited to him as righteousness, a faith prepared to take costly action. It is, of course, hard for us to imagine such a situation, for we would never interpret such a command as the voice of God. However, given a world where child sacrifice happened, for Abraham it was clearly a massive and costly step of obedient faith, and we can imagine how much his trust in God grew through the whole experience.

Clearly these are two different perspectives; but they complement each other. Our actions do not bring us peace with God, because we are always falling short. We simply have to trust in God's action for us in Jesus

Christ. However, a sign of that trust will be the actions flowing out of it. We become part of a circle between faith and works. Our flawed actions drive us to faith. Our faith issues in action.

Some time ago I was doing a primary school assembly, and to illustrate trust I invited children to come up and be blindfolded, then to allow themselves to fall back after I had promised them I would catch them. Several came up, but none of them managed to do it. Just as I was about to abandon the exercise, one final boy put up his hand, so I invited him to come and attempt it. I had hardly put on the blindfold when he launched himself backwards, and I just caught him before he hit the ground. What enabled him to let go and trust where others had been unable? This boy was my son. He trusted his father and then showed his trust in what he did. Faith is action based on trust. Sometimes the action will be trust itself—as when Jesus says, "The work of God is this: to believe in the one he has sent." (John 6:29). Faith is the way we connect to the unseen God; it connects us to his grace and power; it shows in the action of our lives.

Faith, doubt, and unbelief

Faith needs to keep on growing because it is about trust, which is never static; it is about God, for whom there is always more to understand and experience; it is about experimentation, which is a continual learning. Sometimes, as a discussion exercise, I have given people cards with various faith-related words on, such as certainty, assurance, trust, doubt, unbelief. It is interesting to ask which words are most helpful to faith, and which words are the opposite of faith. For the latter, some are inclined to select doubt or unbelief. However, I would want to say that doubt is a friend of faith. It keeps it real and honest.

A biblical example would be John the Baptist. His early proclamation of the identity of Jesus is unequivocal: "Look, the Lamb of God, who takes away the sin of the world! . . . I have seen and I testify that this is God's Chosen One." (John 1:29, 34). However, he is put in prison, and in the lonely, dark days spent in his cell, doubts began to creep in. It is a much more subdued and questioning John who sends a disciple to ask Jesus, "Are you the one who was to come, or should we expect

someone else?" Compared with his early confident assertion, this looks
like a real moment of doubt. However, he is given an upbeat account of
the things happening through Jesus' ministry, which must have brought
him reassurance and hope (Matthew 11:2–6). The honest expression of
doubt leads to a renewed faith.

In an age when it's not so much that people don't believe anything, it's
that they believe everything, then a certain amount of doubt is essential.
My experience, for instance, of reading a book like *The God Delusion*, by
the atheist Richard Dawkins, is to find myself constantly saying, "I don't
believe that either." There are many differing understandings of God and
in many I choose to be a non-believer. Some take the definition of God
beyond its common meaning, which for me has to include the notion of
a supreme, initiating being, both transcendent and immanent, separate
from human life yet deeply involved in it. There are huge mysteries
involved in understanding and experiencing God's nature, but I believe
a serious line is crossed when God is seen just as a human creation, rather
than a pre-existing, freely choosing being. That, for me, is the line into
unbelief. There will be much that is human in our attempts to describe the
mystery, but there *is* something real we're trying to describe. Yet such are
the depths of these mysteries that doubt and questioning are inevitable
and healthy, leading us into a more mature and stronger faith.

You may know the story of the three blind men feeling different parts
of an elephant. As each one touches a side, a tail, or a trunk, they obviously
draw very different conclusions about the nature of an elephant. It is a
story used to make the point that our grasp of the truth of something
can only be partial or relative. However, the story only works because
there is either a narrator or a character in the story (sometimes a king)
who sees the full reality of an elephant and who can therefore expose the
relativism of the blind men.[71]

For me, this illustrates how significant is the belief in a separate
transcendent being, beyond and before human life. That is the definition
of God which we either believe or we don't. After that, there will be a huge
amount that is human and partial in our understanding and experience.
Christians believe that God has not left himself without witness in the
world, and will look supremely to Jesus Christ and the scriptures for
that revelation. However, there will still be much that is human in our

understanding and interpretation of what has been revealed, and that is why certainty, for me, is never a very helpful word in relation to faith. I do believe God has revealed enough of his character and purpose to give us assurance, and as we step out in faith we experience a participation in the life of God through the Spirit which authenticates what we believe. However, it remains faith, and a living faith will inevitably go through times of doubt when beliefs are tested and refined. Henri Nouwen writes of the movement from illusion to prayer as a journey from false certainties to true uncertainties, leaving behind the easy support system of safe gods for a risky surrender to the God whose love has no limits.[72] Our greatest act of faith is to believe that God can use everything to achieve his purpose of enlarging our capacity to give and receive love.

Arrival and journey

The evangelical tradition that nurtured my early faith put more emphasis on arrival than on journey. It picked up what has been called the "realized eschatology" of John's Gospel and the epistles, which is the bringing of the future into the present, our final destiny into the now. An example would be these words of Jesus recorded by John: "Very truly I tell you, whoever hears my word and believes him who sent me has eternal life and will not be judged but has crossed over from death to life."(John 5:24). Chronologically, judgement, death, and eternal life are all to come, yet these words suggest that faith in Jesus takes us beyond death and judgement into the life of eternity now. Similarly, the apostle Paul writes, "Therefore, if anyone is in Christ, the new creation has come: the old has gone, the new is here!" (2 Corinthians 5:17). These are bold assertions which, at best, give great assurance that these new realities aren't just for some far-off future but begin now. The real change has already happened and we can begin to enter into it. Death and judgement hold no fear and cannot touch the real life that has begun.

It is easy, though, to let such a perspective lead us into a rather super-spiritual place, denying the reality of our lives now. If we have arrived, then there is no need to return to any of the mistakes or wounds of the journey; we just need, by faith, to claim the victory of Christ and stand in our new position. However, that can create an existence split between ideal and reality, promise and actual experience. I came to see that to have the assurance of arrival was to give the confidence to undertake the journey, knowing that even when we encountered pain, darkness, and difficulty, we could always be hopeful of what lay ahead. We have been redeemed, we are a new creation in Christ, so we can take that redemption back into the experiences of our life so far and forward into the challenges of the future. For me, as for many, this has involved understanding family patterns which have left their scars on me, ways of relating or acting that have not been truly loving, fears which need addressing if I am going to step into the fullness of life and service God is putting before me. Sometimes that has been very dark and painful, and I have felt a long way from being a new creation. Yet somehow, God leads us on and we grow in faith and maturity.

Faith through death

My faith came alive at university, and one of the leading Christian speakers on the university circuit at the time was David Watson. His preaching was inspirational for many students, as for the large congregation which grew under his ministry at St Michael le Belfrey in York. He had a profound influence on my own faith and call to the ministry. In 1983 David discovered that he had cancer. He was at the height of an international ministry, with speaking tours and festivals of faith all over the world. In spite of much prayer for healing he died a year later, in February 1984, aged 50.

Apart from the personal sadness many felt—myself included—at the untimely loss of such a gifted and yet warm and human Christian leader, his death raised many issues for the charismatic evangelical constituency in the church, for which he was a leading voice. People couldn't understand why someone so clearly being used by God to renew the church was taken so young. People with prominent healing ministries had prayed for him, and he himself had believed that God was healing him. It turned out not to be—at least in the sense of a physical cure. He himself said, "I think that God does have a purpose in our lives, and it is not measured by the length of our life . . . Actually there is nothing more glorious than to be with Christ for ever . . . "[73] Others, out of their pain, made less helpful statements like, "The devil has killed David Watson," revealing (to my mind) a non-biblical dualism that diminished the power of God and lacked a faith perspective beyond death.

It became quite a moment of sober reflection, particularly for charismatic Christianity, which always carried the risk of an over-certain triumphalism. By contrast, some words David spoke two months before he died were measured and moving:

> The most important lesson I have learnt in these past eleven months of suffering from cancer is that God loves me, is always with me—in the dark as in the light—and that I cannot trust him too much. The best is yet to be, once we have put our lives in Christ.[74]

"I cannot trust him too much . . . The best is yet to be." That is the faith God grows in us, often as much through the dark times as well as the light. Sometimes we will feel caught up in the beauty and love of God, and our life in him will feel certain and secure. Sometimes we will feel confused and afraid, and we will have to hang in there. "Now we see through a glass darkly," says Paul, "but then we shall see face to face. Now we know only in part, but then we shall know fully even as we are fully known." (1 Corinthians 13:12). Until that time it will always be faith.

What will heaven be like? Will the idea of being God's children still feel relevant or will our relationship with God have moved beyond that? Will we finally be grown-up or will growth be an eternal reality? I don't think we can answer those questions this side of death. John the apostle affirms what we are now and is honest about what we do not yet know:

> See what great love the Father has lavished on us, that we should be called children of God! And that is what we are! . . . Dear friends, now we are children of God, and what we will be has not yet been made known. But we know that when Christ appears, we shall be like him, for we shall see him as he is.
>
> *1 John 3:1–2*

By faith we are children of God. We are agnostic about what we will be. But we know we shall be like Christ, and that is a maturity we can anticipate with great excitement and hope.

For further thought and discussion

- How would you answer someone who says to you, "I wish I had your faith"?
- How important is faith in realizing the promises of God? In what ways can we make it too important?
- In your experience do we make faith too intellectual or not thoughtful enough? In the church is there too much teaching and not enough action, or is it the other way round?
- What is your response to words like "certainty", "assurance", "doubt", "unbelief"? Do you have a word or phrase that sums up the nature of faith?
- Do you find the idea of "arrival" or "journey" most helpful in describing your Christian life?
- What do you look forward to once we become like Christ and see God face to face?

Afterword

I began with the personal story of my headmaster challenging the sixteen-year-old me to grow up. He made it sound simple, but as I have reflected on it I think that is far from being the case. It is also, to some degree, an unfinished task. We go through life and shoulder greater responsibilities. However, once we reach a certain age we have to assume new dependencies: "... when you are old you will stretch out your hands, and someone else will dress you and lead you where you do not want to go." (John 21:18).

Recently I went on the longest retreat I have ever undertaken, four weeks in silence doing the Ignatian Spiritual Exercises. On previous retreats I have sometimes had a moment when I have broken through to a new experience of God, which has been full of intense joy at his grace and love. On this occasion it never happened like that. I was initially disappointed, but felt God gave me some insight through the parable of the lost son(s). I sensed God saying to me something along the lines of, "You have experienced the party. You cannot keep going back to being a returning prodigal. What about the joy of being a responsible son?"

It opened up some important areas for meditation. It was true, of course, that I now carried much more responsibility in my ministry and family and community. However, in Jesus' parable there is no happy ending for the responsible son. His fate is left hanging as he spurns the celebration party for his returning younger brother, and we are not told what happens after that. Does that suggest responsibility inevitably makes life become more serious and burdensome, less carefree and joyful? That didn't seem like a gospel conclusion but this parable, at least, didn't offer an alternative vision. So I was left to imagine the sequel.

The Return of the Older Son

The older son woke up the next morning feeling angry and sad. He hadn't slept well. The noise from the party echoed inside him long after it had actually finished, and for a while he lay there thinking that he couldn't be bothered to start work that day. He did, of course, because that's what he always did, but the thought had been there and it was a disturbing one, for without work there was no knowing what the space would reveal.

On the way to the cowshed he passed his father, who smiled and muttered something about one less mouth to feed. He frowned, assuming that his father really meant "one *more* mouth to feed", which served to bring back all the feelings about his brother from the night before. It was only when he got to the shed that the penny dropped, as he was confronted by the vacant stall which the calf he had nurtured no longer occupied. The emptiness hit him like a punch in the stomach. He caught his breath and then held it in an attempt to stifle the pain emerging from his guts. All his care and hard work gone in one evening's madness over an irresponsible brother!

The day passed with uneasy silences, at least between the two brothers. His father put his younger son to work straightaway, and then was just around in the background, taking lunch out to him and his brother in the fields to save them having to make the walk home. In truth he had never really done lunch breaks, usually grabbing something and then eating it as he continued work. There was a lot of conversation and banter between his father and brother as they caught up on the previous months, and he didn't hang around too long before resuming work.

As the days passed, life on the farm got harder. The famine that had been in the surrounding areas now began to affect them as well, and they needed each other more and more to work the reluctant land. He had to concede that there was a new work ethic he hadn't seen before in his younger brother, who also had a relaxed and happy relationship with his father. "I can't believe just how good it is working here," his brother often said; "Dad is so generous and encouraging." Though he added, "But anything has to be better than working with those pigs!" The very memory seemed to fire him through even the most stressful day.

He didn't cope well with his brother's enthusiasm. He resented it and envied it at the same time. Then one day, during the lunch break, his younger brother said something along the same lines just once too often. At that moment he exploded: "Oh, it's easy for you to say that, but you weren't here when it was really bad. You'd gone off with half our money, and left all the work to those of us still here. You didn't have to watch Father walking up that hill each day and just standing there. He never said anything but I knew he was looking for you, wondering if perhaps one day he would catch sight of you returning home. Day after day he would return disappointed, and I thought he couldn't do with me kicking off as well. I just had to keep going and make sure we didn't go under. So I tried to do the work of us both, to save him any more worries. It was hard, but better than everything collapsing completely."

It had been said, and not before time. It was his father who broke the silence that followed. "My son," he kept repeating. "My son, I'm so sorry. Yes, I was looking out for your brother. I hoped one day he would come home. That's how parents feel. But never for one moment was I not aware of you as well. You've been brilliant. I was so grateful for how you just got on with things. I worried about you too, and all the extra responsibility you were carrying. But I thought we were in this together. Everything here is as much yours as mine."

The ice had been broken. The wounds were still raw, but a tiny measure of healing had begun. Resentment could not drive him for ever. Gradually he began to tolerate and even appreciate having his brother around again, and he looked forward to the lunch breaks with their father when they could catch up, share concerns, or just be together.

One day he was returning home from working at the far end of the estate when for a moment he thought he could hear music coming from the house. However, as he got near all was quiet, and he assumed it was, perhaps, some of the servants singing as they went about their duties. Yet just as he passed the front door of the house it was flung open and a great cheer went up, with bursts of enthusiastic applause and cries of, "He's a jolly good fellow!" He looked in to see a room full of all his family and friends—well, not huge numbers of friends because he'd always been too busy to keep up with them, but certainly more than he might have expected.

Before he could take it all in, his father spoke above the noise. "My son," he said, "we've been through difficult times. When your brother was away you had to shoulder double the responsibility. Then since he came back, the famine's been hard and we've all had to pull together as best we could. You have kept going. You've worked hard through all this time, and it is in no small measure through what you've done that we have survived and are here today. So when my servant told me that my son had asked for a party I was delighted to agree, because I just want to say, 'Well done!' I have always been ready to throw a party for you and your friends, but until now you've never asked."

There was a pause and everyone held their breath, as they weren't sure how he was going to react because, in truth, he wasn't a party animal. "But," he said, looking puzzled, "but I didn't ask for a party." Everyone looked a bit shocked and, for a moment, feared that it was all about to go wrong. Then the servant spoke up. "No, it was *that* son who asked for a party," he said, pointing at the younger brother; "a surprise party for his brother, just like the one that had been thrown for him." The younger son grinned, a bit sheepishly, before going to put his arm around his brother and saying, "Thanks, bro, for everything. And if Dad has any problems with the cost, then this one is on me."

Dad didn't have any problems with the cost. Returning sons were worth every penny of celebration in his reckoning, whether returning from a far country, or from a hurt, resentful, and locked-away place inside them. Sometimes the latter could be the harder journey home, but the older son was making it. He was discovering that there was a joy in shared responsibility: different from the joy of a returning prodigal but nonetheless real. There was a joy in anyone lost being found—like those friendships that were rekindled at the party. There was space for celebration and gratitude. As he lay down to sleep that night, he felt more hopeful than he had for a long time. He didn't have to be responsible on his own. He still had a father and a brother who shared it with him. However, he did worry that it was now his turn to give the next party.

Notes

1   Richard Dawkins, *The God Delusion* (Bantam, 2006), pp. 403–4. Reprinted by permission of Houghton Mifflin Harcourt Publishing Company and Penguin Random House UK. All rights reserved.

2   Cat Stevens, "Music" (1974).

3   Alan Jamieson, *A Churchless Faith: Faith Journeys Beyond the Churches* (SPCK, 2002), p. 11. Reproduced with permission of SPCK through PLSclear. Jamieson researches the faith journeys of those who have left evangelical, Pentecostal, and charismatic churches.

4   *Mission-shaped Church* (Church House Publishing, 2004) identifies the "de-churched" as 40% of the population, comprising "open de-churched" and "closed de-churched" groups.

5   *Church Times*, 27 April 2018, p. 15. Used by permission.

6   *Church Times*, 4 May 2018, p. 14. Used by permission.

7   Matthew 11:25.

8   Peter Scazzero, *Emotionally Healthy Spirituality* (Thomas Nelson, 2006).

9   From the carol, "Once in royal David's city".

10 Mark Yaconelli, *Contemplative Youth Ministry: Practising the Presence of Jesus with Young People* (SPCK, 2006), p. 68. Reproduced with permission of SPCK through PLSclear.

11 Graham Cray, quoted in David Hilborn and Matt Bird (eds), *God and the Generations: Youth, Age and the Church Today* (Paternoster, 2002), p. 178.

12 Peter Wagner, quoted in Hilborn and Bird, 2002, p. 189.

13 Yaconelli, *Contemplative Youth Ministry*, p. 15. Reproduced with permission of SPCK through PLSclear.

14 Anthony Horowitz, "Odd couples", *The Times* (*Saturday Review*), 26 August 2017, p. 10.

[15] William Wordsworth, "Ode: Intimations of Immortality", from *Recollections of Early Childhood.*

[16] Simone Weil, *Waiting on God* (Routledge, 2009), p. 81. Used with permission.

[17] Marcus Borg, *The Heart of Christianity: Rediscovering a Life of Faith* (Zondervan, 2009), ch. 6.

[18] Dave Tomlinson, *The Bad Christian's Manifesto: Reinventing God (and other modest proposals)* (Hachette UK, 2014), p. 92.

[19] Walter Brueggemann, *Genesis: Interpretation, A Bible Commentary for Teaching and Preaching* (John Knox Press, 1982), pp. 40, 52, 53–4. All italics are Brueggemann's.

[20] Jean-Jacques Suurmond, *Word and Spirit at Play: Towards a Charismatic Theology* (SCM, 1994), p. 35. Reproduced with permission of Hymns Ancient and Modern Ltd through PLSclear.

[21] Benjamin R. Barber, *Consumed: How Markets Corrupt Children, Infantilize Adults, and Swallow Citizens Whole* (W. W. Norton, 2007).

[22] Ben Elton, *Blind Faith* (Black Swan, 2007), pp. 38–39.

[23] M. Scott Peck, *The Road Less Travelled: A New Psychology of Love, Traditional Values and Spiritual Growth* (Arrow Books, 1990), p. 66.

[24] David Hare, *Racing Demon* (Faber & Faber, 1990), p. 1.

[25] *Common Worship: Daily Prayer* (Church House Publishing, 2005).

[26] Jonathan Sacks outlines five key losses arising from collective and individual loss of faith: the belief in human dignity and the sanctity of life, collective responsibility for the common good, morality, marriage, and the possibility of a meaningful life. Jonathan Sacks, *The Great Partnership: God, Science and the Search for Meaning* (Hachette, 2011), p. 101.

[27] Sacks, *The Great Partnership*, p. 24. Used by permission of Hodders and Penguin Random House.

[28] *Common Worship: Services and Prayers for the Church of England* (Church House Publishing, 2000), p. 409. Common Worship material is © The Archbishops' Council, 2000, and is reproduced by permission. All rights reserved. copyright@churchofengland.org.

[29] As John Hick puts it, "On the one hand, then, we should expect the reality of God to be other than automatically and undeniably evident to us; it will, on the contrary, be possible for our minds to rest in the world itself without passing beyond it to its Maker. But we should also expect the reality of God to become evident to men in so far as they are willing to live as creatures in

the presence of an infinitely perfect Being whose very existence sets them under a sovereign claim of worship and obedience . . . Thus the world, as the environment of man's life, will be religiously ambiguous, both veiling God and revealing Him—veiling Him to ensure man's freedom and revealing Him to men as they rightly exercise that freedom." John Hick, *Evil and the God of Love* (Macmillan, 1966), p. 318.

30   Anthony Bloom, *School for Prayer* (Darton, Longman & Todd, 1970), p. 2.

31   See, for example, St John of the Cross, *Ascent of Mount Carmel*, <https://www.ecatholic2000.com/stjohn/ascent.shtml>, and *Dark Night of the Soul*, <http://www.carmelitemonks.org/Vocation/DarkNight-StJohnoftheCross.pdf> (accessed 12 November 2018).

32   Ruth Burrows OCD, *Guidelines for Mystical Prayer* (Sheed & Ward, 1976), pp. 38–9.

33   It is an understanding conveyed in a line from the popular song "How deep the Father's love for us" by Stuart Townend: "The Father turns His face away". There is a strand of evangelical theology that is very wedded to "penal substitution" as the foundational theory of the atonement. It is certainly a theory that can be argued from the scriptures (alongside others). However, I would claim that it is fatally undermined if expressed in the clumsy and insensitive way of some piety which really portrays God as an abusive or indifferent father. At a recent service I attended, we sang, "Now why this fear and unbelief? Has not the Father put to grief His spotless Son for us?" (adapted by Doug Plank from Augustus Toplady's hymn "From whence this fear and unbelief?"). It's a terrible image, which requires too much mental gymnastics to be reconciled with a loving God who himself bears the pain of our indifference.

34   From Charles Wesley's hymn "And can it be?".

35   From an article by Sister Mary Magdalen that appeared in Issue 118 of *Renewal Magazine*, copyright Premier Christian Communications Ltd. www.premier.org.uk. Used with permission.

36   Romans 10:14–15.

37   "Oh, the bitter shame and sorrow" by Theodore Monod.

38   Often attributed to Teresa of Avila, but not found in her writings.

39   Lyrics by John du Prez and Eric Idle, based on the hymn by Cecil Frances Alexander; <http://www.montypython.net/scripts/allthing.php> (accessed 13 November 2018).

[40] David E. Jenkins, *God, Miracle and the Church of England* (SCM, 1987), p. 5.

[41] Richard Bauckham, "Providence", <http://richardbauckham.co.uk/uploads/Accessible/Providence.pdf>, p. 2 (accessed 13 November 2018).

[42] Quoted by Simon Tugwell OP in his *Prayer in Practice* (Templegate, 1974), p. 21.

[43] Jenkins, *God, Miracle and the Church of England*, p. 6. Reproduced with permission of Hymns Ancient and Modern Ltd through PLSclear.

[44] C. S. Lewis, *The Problem of Pain* (Fontana Books, 1957), p.vii. © CS Lewis Pte Ltd 1940. Used with permission.

[45] Alister McGrath, *The Intellectual Origins of the European Reformation* (Blackwell, 1992), pp. 139ff.

[46] *The Book of Common Prayer*: "The Order for the Visitation of the Sick".

[47] Statistics quoted by the mental health charity Mind, <https://www.mind.org.uk> (accessed 13 November 2018).

[48] Viktor E. Frankl, *Man's Search for Meaning* (Rider, 2004), p. 109.

[49] <http://www.emmaus.org.uk/history> (accessed 13 November 2018).

[50] M. Scott Peck, *The Road Less Traveled: A New Psychology of Love, Traditional Values and Spiritual Growth* (Simon & Schuster, 1978).

[51] Anthony Bloom, *Beginning to Pray* (Paulist Press, 1970), p. 6.

[52] C. S. Lewis, *The Horse and His Boy* (HarperCollins, 1980), p. 130. © CS Lewis Pte Ltd 1954. Used with permission.

[53] Anecdote based on a passage in Winston Churchill, *Thoughts and Adventures* (Butterworth, 1932), p. 113.

[54] Charles Handy, *The Elephant and the Flea: New Thinking for a New World* (Random House, 2002), p. 32.

[55] Robin Skynner and John Cleese, *Families and How to Survive Them* (Methuen, 1983), p. 185. Reproduced by permission of The Random House Group Ltd. © 1983.

[56] Quoted in David Clines, "Sin and Maturity", in *Third Way* magazine, November 1980, pp. 8–10, at p. 9.

[57] Martin L. Smith, *A Season for the Spirit* (Fount, 1991), p. 83. Reproduced by permission of The Random House Group Ltd. © 1983.

[58] Brother Lawrence, *The Practice of the Presence of God* (Allenson, 1906), pp. 22–23 (author's italics).

[59] John V. Taylor, *The Christlike God* (SCM, 1992), p. 76.

[60] John R. W. Stott, *Baptism and Fullness: The Work of the Holy Spirit Today* (IVP, 1975), p. 15. Reproduced with permission of The Inter-Varsity Press Ltd through PLSclear.

[61] Defining the boundaries of human sexuality is currently the big issue in the church, causing great division and potential schism. It would certainly be helpful to know what the grown-up Jesus might have felt about such matters and how we might begin to discern his mind today. It feels too big a subject to open up here, but I refer you to Jayne Ozanne (ed.), *Journeys in Grace and Truth: Revisiting Scripture and Sexuality* (Via Media, 2016), where I and others seek to grapple with scripture and experience on this issue.

[62] Lesslie Newbigin, *The Gospel in a Pluralist Society* (Eerdmans/WCC, 1989, pp. 227, 231. Reproduced with permission of SPCK through PLSclear.

[63] Greg Haslam, "Do I really need to go to church?", <http://www.eauk.org/idea/do-i-really-need-to-go-to-church.cfm> (September 2014, accessed 19 November 2018). Used with permission of the Evangelical Alliance.

[64] Canons of the Church of England, C 15, Of the Declaration of Assent.

[65] John Boyne, *The Boy in the Striped Pyjamas* (Black Swan, 2007), pp. 180–181.

[66] See, for example, the Church Mission Society website: <https://churchmission society.org/resources/dwelling-word> (accessed 20 November 2018).

[67] Paul Bayes, quoting Walter J. Hollenweger's *Evangelism Today*, in Ozanne (ed.), *Journeys of Grace and Truth*, p. 1. Used with permission.

[68] Vincent J. Donovan, *Christianity Rediscovered: An Epistle from the Masai* (Fides/Claretian, 1978), pp. 33–38 (author's italics). Reproduced with permission of Hymns Ancient and Modern Ltd through PLSclear.

[69] Galatians 2:15–16, Romans 3:21–24.

[70] Rick Warren, *The Purpose Driven Life* (Zondervan, 2002), p. 231 (author's italics).

[71] Cf. Newbigin, *The Gospel in a Pluralist Society*, p. 9.

[72] Henri J. M. Nouwen, *Reaching Out: The Three Movements of the Spiritual Life* (Fount, 1980), p. 117.

[73] Transcript of a BBC Radio 4 interview in April 1983 from St Michael le Belfrey Church, York.

[74] Ibid.